THE
ARTISTIC
EDGE

*7 Skills Children Need to Succeed in
an Increasingly Right Brain World*

LISA PHILLIPS

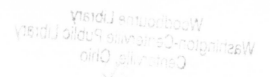

The Artistic Edge

7 Skills Children Need to Succeed in an Increasingly Right Brain World

Copyright © 2012 by Lisa Phillips. All rights reserved.

ISBN: 978-0-9917302-0-9

Requests to the publisher should be addressed to:

Lisa Phillips
Canada's Academy of Stage and Studio Arts
124 Merton Street, Suite 403
Toronto, ON M4S 2Z2
416-558-0922

The Artistic Edge
info@theartisticedge.ca
www.theartisticedge.ca

DEDICATION

To all the children of the world:

Know that you are full of boundless potential, capable of achieving extraordinary things.

My wish for you is that each of you finds a role model who will help you see that potential within yourself.

You have incredible gifts and talents. Imagine what your life, and the world, would be like if you realized them.

CONTENTS

FOREWORD

When Lisa approached me to write the Foreword for her book, I was thrilled to do it. As a parent, grandparent and author of *The New York Times* bestseller, *Chicken Soup for the Parent's Soul*, I knew the message of her book was extremely important.

As parents, we strive to give the best to our children. We love and care for them and teach them skills we think they need to be successful in life. However, we are not the only ones guiding them through the challenges of growing up. A large majority of our children's time is spent interacting with other adults— school teachers, babysitters, piano teachers, swim instructors, other friends' parents and so on. As much as we wish we could, we can't always control the messages being given to our children.

The Artistic Edge highlights how important the arts are for the future of our children. The world is a competitive place and many young people today are clearly not ready for it. Outlined in this book are seven skills that are developed through the arts that are crucial for the success of our children. Every teacher, parent, arts professional, or in fact anyone with a vested interest in the future of our children must read this book!

I first met Lisa at a coaching seminar I was facilitating in Toronto in November 2011. What struck me right away was her passion for, and brilliance in, working with young people. It was clear how dedicated she was to their growth and development. It was also clear that she would stop at nothing to ensure her dreams became reality. She is the type of role model we want for our children.

As the nation's #1 success and investment coach, I know what it takes to succeed in business. Over the years I have had many business ventures. Some have been huge successes and others were lessons learned. What I have come to realize is that there are two key ingredients that entrepreneurs need to be successful: creativity and leadership.

It frightens me to think that young people are finishing school with both of these skills so underdeveloped. *The Artistic Edge* explains how these skills can be nurtured through the arts, giving our children a competitive advantage that will help to ensure greater success as they move into adulthood.

What resonates so strongly for me is the discussion about mindset in chapter six. As one of 40 teachers in the world filmed for the hit movie sensation, *The Secret*, I can tell you without doubt that your thoughts shape your reality. How you view challenges in your life and the choices you make during those obstacles carve the life you will have.

So what kind of life do we want for our children? I can only speak for myself, but I will do anything to ensure that my children and grandchildren have every opportunity to achieve success. Success is not handed to us on a silver platter. I didn't end up in the *Canadian Who's Who* List by sitting idly by and waiting for success to show up at my doorstep. I worked extremely hard for it. I learned from experts, focused on developing my strengths and I persevered when faced with challenges.

The reality is that most people struggle to achieve success. Why? This is because they don't want to put in the work. As parents, it is our job to equip our children with all the skills they need, and to teach them that work ethic so they are prepared for the realities of life after school. Lisa's book explores how to develop creativity and leadership skills that our children need now. Education in the arts is not just for those who want to pursue careers in the arts. It is about helping our children develop the skill set they need most in the twenty-first century. *The Artistic Edge* will help you give it to them. Their success in life depends on it!

Raymond Aaron
New York Times Bestselling Author
www.UltimateAuthorBootcamp.com

ACKNOWLEDGEMENTS

I am the first person to admit that I cannot achieve great things alone. Just as it takes a village to raise a child, it takes a village to turn dreams into reality. I am truly grateful to the people in my life who have taken the time to help me on my journey of creating this book.

- I thank my mother and sister, Susan and Nicky Phillips, for their unfailing love and support. Their words and actions define the true meaning of family. Everyone should be so lucky to have family like them in their life.

- I thank my Director of Programming, Rosie Kerr, for all of her ideas and hours of brainstorming and editing. I am so grateful for all her assistance in making this book a reality. I look forward to many more years of success as we work together in bringing the arts and leadership to children.

- I thank Manon Pinard, who is like a second sister to me. She has taught me so much about leadership and dealing with conflict. Her support of my endeavours over the past few years means a great deal to me.

- I thank my aunt, Janet Jundler, for her hours of editing, support and guidance. Her students are lucky to have such a dedicated and talented English teacher.

- I thank Fran Bleviss, for her assistance in editing the book on such short notice.
- I thank my friends and colleagues at Camp Tawingo, Mike and Tia Pearse and John "Jorgi" Jorgenson, for being such a support early on in my camping career and for their on-going support of Horizon Arts Camp.
- I thank Michael Brandwein for teaching me how important the job of a camp director truly is and what an opportunity we have as camp professionals to make a difference in the lives of young people. Please visit his website: **www.michaelbrandwein.com**
- I thank Raymond Aaron for writing the Foreword to my book and for his ongoing guidance and support.
- I thank my dear friend, David Roa, for pushing me to always see the best in myself. I haven't met many people in my life who are as driven as he and I, and I look forward to sharing our successes for many years to come.
- I thank my father, the late Dr. David Phillips, for instilling a love of the arts in me. One of my strongest memories of my dad is how he woke us up every morning by blasting musical theatre music through the house instead of using an alarm clock. I miss him every day, and I am proud to say that his love of the arts lives on in both his children.
- I thank all of the campers and staff with whom I have worked with over the years. I have learned a great deal from them, and I thank them for the moments we have shared at camp together.

CHAPTER ONE

THE AUDITION

It seems fitting to tell you that when I started writing this book I began with chapter six, the chapter that stresses that "Anything Is Possible." I had always wanted to write a book. In fact, for years I started stories with the intention of turning them into novels. I even took a children's book writing course once. I guess I never really had the right topic until now. Why did I start with chapter six? I think I needed to remind myself that it was finally possible for me to have a published book. So why not start writing the chapter that is meant to remind all of us that dreams can turn into reality when we have the focus and drive to make it so?

My career in the arts has been varied, with experiences in musical theatre, dance, film and television. I think the importance of my experiences in these art forms became more apparent to me as I started working more intensely with children. I have been working with children in the arts and leadership for sixteen years and I am going into my tenth year as a camp director. I have to say that the trends I have begun to see emerge from the current generation concern me. Young people today seem to be growing up with more stresses and more challenges than children had to deal with when I grew up. The concerning part is, they seem less prepared to handle the pressure.

Life is like an audition. Just as a performer presents a song or monologue in front of a casting director, young people present their choices, ideas and achievements in front of their parents, teachers and bosses who all determine what part they get. Are they cast as the go-getting over-achiever who will stop at nothing to achieve their goals or the lazy couch potato who has never put the effort into realizing their full potential? Or are they somewhere in between?

For those of you involved in the arts, you know that it takes a lot of preparation to get ready for an audition. You have to choose a piece that makes you stand out, memorize lines, understand the character's back story and master the technique to deliver your piece flawlessly. Not only do you have to win over your audition panel, but you have to stand out over your competition. Life is no different. So if we want our young people to succeed in life, they need to prepare for life just as they would for an audition.

Life can be challenging, and growing up is not always easy. Young people are confronted with a lot of pressure.

There is pressure to…

- look a certain way.
- fit in with the cool crowd.
- get into the best schools.
- have the latest electronic gadget/phone.
- get a great job.
- make a lot of money.
- have a lot of friends.
- have the right friends.
- be happy.
- be perfect.
- be successful.
- please everyone (friends, parents, teachers etc.).

Sure, those pressures existed when I was growing up, too, but they have been magnified ten-fold by the technological advances of the internet and sophisticated marketing—so much so that young people are in a constant race to keep up. They are caught up in a mad dash to acquire all the things that will take their social status to ultimate heights. As adults try to help young people in this quest, they have forgotten our children need to learn leadership skills to allow them to achieve all the successes they desire in life.

Why aren't kids ready to face all that pressure? I believe it is because they have not spent enough time practicing the skills they need to meet the pressures life throws at them. There is a major disconnect between the knowledge they absorb at school and their ability to use that knowledge. The missing piece, I believe, is leadership skills.

Knowing how to conjugate a verb or solve a quadratic equation is not going help kids achieve all the goals on their pressure list. I am not saying that academic knowledge is not important. Of course it is. However, children need much more than just academic skills to be successful in today's world. Leadership and life skills are the tools that teach children how to function practically in the world, to transform their dreams into reality and to leave a legacy.

So, what if every child had the confidence to handle all of life's challenges? Wouldn't we feel so much better if we knew we had given our children the skills they need to be as successful and happy as they can be in their adult lives? How are parents and educators going to equip their children with the tools to overcome roadblocks and launch them on the path to success?

The answer is simple - the arts.

Engaging in music, dance, theatre or visual arts provides young people with the competitive edge they need to achieve success in every aspect of their lives. You are probably asking yourself, "How do the arts do that?" The arts teach countless skills that give children the tools, not only to make it to their audition, but to land their dream part as well.

The Artistic Edge is about how to set young people up on a path to success given the current state of the world. I believe, as educators, we are falling short because we have not fully adapted to the way the world is changing. We are still acting as if competition for jobs is local, the way it used to be, rather than global, the way it really is now. Our children will be competing for jobs, not only against other people in their hometown—or even in their home country—but against workers in every corner of the world.

Competition is fierce and we are not preparing kids to be adaptable and creative in the ways they need to be in order to cope with the quickly shifting marketplace. According to a 2011 report by the *Conference Board of Canada*, the skills required for today's workforce are critical thinking and creativity, problem-solving skills, effective communication, and the ability to adapt and learn throughout one's career. Today's business leaders agree that arts training can help prepare our young people for any career choice. Warren Goldring, co-founder of the Canadian investment company *AGR Management*, gave this advice, "Don't overlook education in the arts. There has been a tendency for students today to study the hard sciences, business, or computers. An arts training will provide the ability to think logically and that's the commodity that is in the shortest supply in business ... studying the arts will develop skills that can help you in any career."

> " *Leadership is the capacity to translate vision into reality.*
> ~**Warren G. Bennis**~

WORRYING TRENDS

Looking back over my years of experience working with young people, I see some consistent weaknesses in important skill areas. Unless these skills are sufficiently developed and practiced as they grow up, young people's chances of success will be severely limited.

What I see in young people:

- They have difficulty communicating, especially in a work context.
- They rarely take responsibility for their mistakes.
- They struggle to maintain a strong and consistent work ethic.
- They get stuck when faced with a problem, because the challenges seem insurmountable.
- They lack confidence.
- They are overstressed, and they lack the tools to find balance.
- They are not willing to put in the work necessary to achieve their dreams.

Wow, that sounds pretty grim. Let me be clear, not every young person has all these limitations. Some young people may not have any, but the above challenges represent a definite trend that can easily be found in the current generation.

In our society, more often than not, we are told that we cannot do something, rather than being encouraged to try. So, it is no wonder we all walk around in a state of total apprehension at the thought of trying something new or attempting a bold choice. "What if we can't do it?" Best not to try all, just in case we fail. Most people exist their whole lives with this mindset. How terribly sad, that there is incredible talent just beneath the surface just waiting to flourish. Instead it fades away, along with the potential for an incredible life and contribution to the world. I hope this book will show that it is through practicing the necessary skills that anyone can achieve big dreams!

7 SKILLS TO SET YOUNG PEOPLE ON A PATH TO SUCCESS

Many experts say that it is creative thinking and innovation that are needed to land the most coveted jobs. I agree, but I also see a whole skill set, in addition to creativity, that is crucial for young people to develop in order to find success in life.

I have identified seven skills young people can learn from the arts that will equip them to compete. Here is a brief outline of the skills you will read about in the upcoming chapters:

Skill # 1

Creative Thinking: Thinking creatively is about learning to think with your 'right brain' so that you are able to see problems in a 'big picture' way and find innovative solutions to them. In chapter three, I will explore how the current job market trends are identifying the need for creativity from the emerging workforce.

Skill #2

Confidence: Instilling self-confidence in our children is one of the most important things that we can do to help them be successful as adults. Too often we do just the opposite. In chapter four, I will look at the ways in which the arts can help to counteract the tendencies of adults to reinforce kids' fears and undermine their confidence.

Skill #3

Problem-Solving: Adults also inadvertently tend to encourage kids to accept failure as an option rather than teaching them effective problem-solving skills. In chapter five, I will explain how the arts can build children's abilities to see problems as creative opportunities instead of as obstacles.

Skill #4

Dreaming Big: There is a balance to be struck between acknowledging the reality of limits and refusing to give up on big dreams. In chapter six, I will detail the importance of finding that balance and holding on to dreams, as well as how the arts can be extremely effective in showing young people how to achieve that balance.

Skill #5

Accountability & Relationship Building: Our culture often enables kids to sidestep responsibility for their actions, and that lack of accountability is the first step on the road to poor professional relationships and lack of career success. In chapter seven, I will discuss how training in the arts teaches young people how to take responsibility for the things they do and build positive relationships that will ensure success.

Skill #6

Communication: Thanks to technology, today's young people are falling behind older generations in the development of strong communication skills. In chapter eight, I will outline how the arts can give kids the communication skills that they are not learning from their high-tech tools.

Skill #7

Adaptability: The world is changing quickly, and perhaps no skill is more crucial to young people's future success than the ability to adapt to those changes as they happen. In chapter nine, I will talk about how the arts will make young people more flexible and more successful at confronting the new challenges that our rapidly changing world will put in front of them.

GENERATION Z

The current generation, known as Generation Z or the Net Generation, was born from the mid-1990s to the present. Highly skilled with technology, this group of young people has never been without the internet, text messaging, MP3 players or the latest smartphones. They are highly connected with their peers, and they interact through countless social media platforms like *Facebook* and *Twitter*. Even though these advances in technology allow for incredibly innovative ways for people to connect, there still seems to be a lack of quality in the communication itself.

So who is Generation Z?

Technology-Minded: The aptly named Net Generation has never known a time when information, music and games were not instantly available. They are used to instant gratification in everything and have no trouble expressing their displeasure when they don't get exactly what they want.

Transparency: This is the most open and outspoken generation in history. They say what they think and feel, and they expect the same from others. They feel entitled to have the answers to all of their questions, even when the questions are of a personal nature.

Creative and Curious: This is a colourful and expressive generation. They have huge ideas about how to express themselves to the world, and they have a need for their talents to be recognized. It is our role to help them harness and direct this!

Environmentally and Globally Aware: With so much information instantly available, these young people are always aware of what is happening in the world. They see more, and want to do more to help the world than ever before.

Inclusive: Generation Z is rapidly becoming known as the most inclusive generation in history. They have internet friends from all different backgrounds around the world, and they are more likely to look for similarities than differences when meeting new people.

To summarize, although I have spoken about the limitations of Generation Z, there is much that is positive about today's young people. This new generation embodies all of the individuality prized by Generation X coupled with the acceptance and social attitudes of Generation Y. Though people from older generations frown about lowered attention spans, over-sharing and incessant texting, there can be no denying the fact that Generation Z has some serious star power. They are driven by a fierce sense of entitlement and equality, leading them to demand accountability in media, politics and marketing like never before. However, this same sense of entitlement sometimes prevents them from seeing how their actions can negatively impact those around them.

The question is, how will the current generation behave in the workplace? What kind of workers will they be? The evidence seems to suggest that there will be both positive and negative aspects of Generation Z that will influence how they deal with responsibilities, co-workers and employers. Their experience with technology is going to make them smart, able to process information quickly and become excellent information gatherers.

Unfortunately, there could be a downside. Their poor communication skills and self-focused reliance on technology could make them unsuccessful team players. In addition, their need for instant gratification could prevent them from becoming persistent, effective problem-solvers.

THE ROLE OF PARENTS AND EDUCATORS

What can we do to help? As their parents, we can try to find a balance between encouraging our children to face challenges head-on and trying to protect them from failure and disappointment. We can try not to be 'helicopter parents' — those parents who hover over their children, trying to deflect anything difficult that might come their way.

"There are parents who will not say no to their child because they truly believe this is bad for their child to hear," writes Dr. Maggie Mamen, author of *The Pampered Child Syndrome: How to Recognize It, How to Manage It, and How to Avoid It.* Many parents recognize the intense pressure young people face in the twenty-first century and their instinct is to shield them from it as much as they can. They have a tendency to solve problems for their children, instead of teaching them how to do it for themselves.

Helicopter parents are not helping their children develop leadership skills. Instead, they are doing too many things for their children and robbing them of the chance to develop their own skills and talents.

Of course, parents want to give their kids the right preparation for the future, but since the world is changing so rapidly, they are not always sure how to do it. In my opinion, the role of the parent is that of a coach — someone who gives encouragement and advice, and teaches both hard and soft skills, but does not do the work for the child. They guide them through each challenge, and as they get more proficient, they push them to try things that are more and more difficult.

As educators, we need to guide young people toward developing the skills they will need to be successful. We need to know who they are, what their strengths are, and what their challenges are. Ultimately, we need to know how to take all of that knowledge and give them the tools they need to become their best self.

The Artistic Edge aims to find the solution to the challenges of educating Generation Z. It will do so by examining how the arts develop the skills young people will need to move confidently and successfully into the future. The world is competitive, and our children are not competing as well as they could be. This book explores how we can provide our children with a competitive edge, by giving them an artistic one!

CHAPTER TWO

THE LEFT BRAIN, RIGHT BRAIN DIFFERENCE

How the Arts Develop New Ways of Thinking

We all have an enormous capacity to learn, but how well we develop that capacity depends on how we learn to use our brains. We absorb an amazing amount of information during our lives, and how we make use of that information is what provides us with opportunities and successes. Rena Upitis, a Professor of Education at *Queen's University* and a leading expert in arts education in Canada says, "Existing brain research suggests that experiences in the arts—particularly extended musical experiences—contribute to a fully functioning brain and body." In this chapter, I will investigate how current research can help us understand how skills we learn in the arts can transfer to other parts of our lives.

LEFT BRAIN OR RIGHT BRAIN?

Increasingly, I have noticed that people are being categorized as either left brain or right brain thinkers. Typically, people categorized as left brainers are the accountants and engineers. They make decisions with facts, not emotions and are said to think logically and analytically. The right brainers, on the other hand, are the creative types. They are said to think intuitively and have the ability to see patterns. They are those who lead with the heart and tend to see the bigger picture of the world around them.

The truth is, all of us use both sides of our brain in almost everything we do. Education consultant Eric Jensen illustrates this when he says, "listening to someone speak may seem like a left-hemisphere activity since the left side processes words, definitions, and language…Contrary to this, however, evidence suggests that the right hemisphere processes the inflection, tonality, tempo, and volume of the communication—elements that are actually more critical to the meaning of a conversation than the words themselves."

In a recent review of neuroscience literature, Rena Upitis explains that there is no scientific evidence that supports a link between creativity and activity in the right side of the brain. She also found that there is no direct evidence to support an analytical, logical thinking style for the left side of the brain. Thus, scientific debate about the connection between the right side of the brain and creativity still continues.

Regardless of this fact, we still use left versus right brain as a social metaphor to describe people's tendencies, differences in skill and ways of thinking. The next chapter highlights the work of Daniel Pink, who describes a future North American workforce that needs to focus on its right brain abilities. What he really means is, in an increasingly global workforce, competition creates a demand for young people with creative thinking skills. In reality, it does not matter which side of the brain creative thinking uses, it matters how well it is developed and how often it is used. Therefore, the left brain versus right brain metaphor is a useful way to talk about the kinds of skills and ways of thinking we want to encourage our children to develop.

THE BRAIN AND LEARNING

We hear from many sources that it is easier for young children to learn foreign languages than it is for adults, and they are right! Children's minds are more flexible than the brains of adults, and they develop new neural connections at an astonishing rate. According to the work of William Greenough, there is strong evidence which suggests that our brains are the most flexible during the first ten years of life. As we age, that ability to create new pathways—which we need in order to set up new language patterns in our brains—is diminished. Eric Jensen in his 2008 article, *A Fresh Look at Brain-Based Education*, highlights research that shows that we never lose the ability to create new pathways. *Neuroplasticity* is the brain's ability to change and adapt throughout our lives. Even though our brains are always changing, learning a new language when you are thirty-five is still more challenging than when you are five.

BONUS

 Scan here to visit *Lumosity* to be introduced to innovative games that develop and train your brain. Or visit: www.theartisticedge.ca/thebook

This is why it is so vital for children to have new experiences and to try new ways of performing tasks when they are younger. The more they do, the more they learn. The more they learn, the more new connections are formed. Forming those new connections allows children to use information in new and different ways, letting them adapt to the ever-changing conditions around us. Upitis says, "...Researchers, teachers and neuroscientists alike agree that a child's brain needs to be stimulated in a variety of ways to foster development."

"When you learn to tie your shoes, ride a bicycle, drive a car, use a computer keyboard, or learn a musical instrument, your brain gradually develops the neural pathways to make your 'practicing' become automatic," says psychologist Thomas A. Richards. In other words, what Richards emphasizes, is that the more we practice a skill the more automatic it becomes.

When we think about education, we normally think about classrooms and listening to a teacher explain or describe something to a class of students. This is one way in which children can learn, but not the only way.

A well-rounded educational program uses components of a variety of learning styles. It also pushes learners to make use of abilities and ways of thinking that may otherwise remain underdeveloped. I myself am very much a visual learner. When I am being taught something in a classroom setting and the instruction is only oral, I struggle to grasp the concept. As soon as I have something visual to look at, my understanding of what is being taught is much clearer and occurs much faster. As I mentioned above, the goal should be to help children to create more connections in their minds, allowing them to make the best possible use of their skill and effort.

MORE THAN ONE WAY TO LEARN—ARTISTIC HABITS OF MIND

In an effort to understand how learning in the arts can be transferred to other contexts, American Education Psychologists began to investigate a concept called *Habits of Mind.* These are ways of thinking that are learned through the creative process.

Arguably, the most important habits of mind fall into the category of self-regulation, which is a set of skills that allows us to regulate our own learning. In other words, paying attention to how well you are learning something. Researchers Susan Baum, Steven Owen, and Barry Oreck found that self-regulation skills learned through the arts include: paying attention, using feedback to improve learning, problem-solving, taking risks, co-operating, and setting goals. These are very important habits of mind that will contribute to success in many other contexts because they teach us how to pay attention to our own learning and how we can best improve.

In another investigation of habits of mind, the book *Studio Thinking: The Real Benefits of Visual Arts Education*, describes the benefits of studying art for high school students. This book identifies eight important habits of mind developed while creating visual art work. These included: reflecting, questioning, explaining, evaluating, persisting, and envisioning.

Participating in the arts help us to slow down and practice all of these key skills. No matter what artistic discipline we are learning, there is always a great deal of reflection and questioning. For example, in theatre we analyze scripts to discover why a character feels a particular way.

The habit of envisioning builds skills in predicting and adapting. This allows us to develop the ability to notice and recognize patterns which in turn can help us predict what is coming and solve problems that may arise. When we practice thinking things through before they happen, we plan more effectively.

I would propose that developing these habits of mind allows students to experiment with many different ways of thinking. It provides them with more tools in their tool box. By using multiple ways of thinking, they forge new connections in their brains, providing them with a more comprehensive skill set that they will be able to use for the rest of their lives.

Artful Thinking, a program developed at *Harvard University*, teaches routines or thinking habits that develop a child's creative thinking. As the name implies, these habits of thinking are developed during learning experiences in the arts. These include: reasoning, exploring multiple view points, questioning and investigation, observing and describing, comparing and connecting new ideas to prior knowledge, and finding complexity.

The habit of comparing and connecting new ideas to prior knowledge is particularly useful in developing creative thinking and adaptability. "How is a raven like a writing desk?" asks the door mouse in *Alice In Wonderland*. They are not alike, as Alice later finds out. Or are they? The arts ask these kinds of seemingly absurd questions to encourage children to find metaphors and connections between concepts. The image below is an excellent example of this.

This award winning advertisement out of Mumbai, India asks the question, how is coffee like an owl? Without words, it links the strength of the coffee to the strength of a wise old owl. To someone else, it might say—if you want to stay up all night, drink this coffee. This kind of comparing and connecting of ideas will serve young people well in a job in marketing or advertising.

It makes sense. If we become used to thinking about things critically, asking questions and connecting meanings across contexts, why wouldn't we apply this thinking to multiple contexts in our lives?

Learning to look at a complex problem or situation is also important. The arts allow us to practice investigating complexity by learning to break down different layers of a given situation. Through the creative process, we develop an understanding of how different aspects of a problem interact with each other, making us effective problem-solvers.

Another important element of the *Artful Thinking* program is exploring multiple viewpoints. Being able to see things from the perspectives of others helps us build relationships and solve problems. It develops empathy and enhances our ability to read others better. We can interpret what they mean, and understand their wants and needs. People want to work with those they can relate to and who can relate to them. Developing this kind of social capital gives us an important tool to utilize in every aspect of life.

As part of a larger arts integration movement, the *Artful Thinking* program trains classroom teachers to encourage these habits, not only in teaching art, but in all subjects across the curriculum. The rise in popularity and funding for arts integration programs in schools throughout Canada and the U.S., shows a growing recognition of the importance of developing these ways of thinking in children's development.

By exploring these various methods of thinking, arts education improves our ability to use our brains. If we have multiple lines of connections working on the same problem, we will find an answer more quickly. We are more likely to "think outside the box" when coming up with a solution. Our mind is firing on all cylinders which is the most efficient and productive way possible to solve problems. All this comes from remembering that we can use more than one way to learn.

WHERE DO WE GO FROM HERE?

In our current educational system, schools blend learning styles to some extent, but physical and social components do not figure as strongly into a student's success. This pattern holds true for many subjects studied at school: English, history, social studies, mathematics, and foreign languages. The class structure and testing requirements tend to favour logical and verbal abilities.

When we teach children only one way to learn and only one way to solve problems, they will use that method regardless of whether or not it is right for every situation. Logical and verbal skills are vital for coping in life, but rounding out children's abilities by teaching them multiple ways of thinking provides them with more ways to succeed. When learning focuses most strongly on multiple ways of thinking, it will affect how children operate as they progress through their classes and, ultimately, throughout their working lives.

When we teach children a variety of ways to learn and to solve problems, they are more confident and adaptable when new situations arise. Developing confidence is crucial since it gives children the courage to try new solutions if old ones no longer work. This truly is the best gift we can give to our children.

In the next chapter, I will look at why the difference between, so called, left brain and right brain thinking is a key to how successful our children will be as they enter careers in the twenty-first century. The world is changing, and an ability to think creatively and conceptually is becoming increasingly important.

The next generation is entering a fiercely competitive job market, and some of the most valuable skills in this new job market are creativity and big-picture thinking. If they are going to compete successfully, our children need to use their whole brains, and be practiced in multiple ways of thinking. Involvement in the arts will get them there.

CHAPTER THREE

REACHING BEYOND THE BOX

Why Thinking Creatively Can Equal a Better Career

A CHANGING WORLD

Many people are talking about an ongoing large-scale shift in the way we get work done. Daniel Pink, author of *The New York Times* bestseller, *A Whole New Mind: Why Right-Brainers Will Rule the Future,* explains the nature of this shift and what it means for the future of North American workers. Pink says we are in the process of shifting from the Information Age to the Conceptual Age, a shift from an economy in which the transfer of information is not as important as the content of the information being transferred. What this means is that much of the left brain, linear work—work that requires the simple processing of information—is being outsourced to foreign workers who can do the work just as well as, but much more cheaply than North American workers.

Outsourcing to foreign workers is becoming more and more common in the Western world. People in India, the Philippines and countless other countries are just as capable as we are. They are university educated with a strong work ethic, and they are highly motivated to compete with North American talent. They are competing and they are winning because, in addition to their education and qualifications, their work costs significantly less. For the same—or sometimes even better—quality of work, companies in Canada and the United States can pay foreign workers 50-70% less than they would have to pay North American workers.

Although the 'offshoring' trend began in the manufacturing sector, the movement of service and information work to other countries has gained steam in recent years. From virtual administrative assistants to graphic designers, foreign information workers are benefitting from an economic environment in which outsourcing is growing at a rapid rate. Why wouldn't a company want to outsource to get work done with less cost?

I have done it myself. When I decided to launch my blog, the precursor to this book, I put a job posting for the website design on elance.com, a well-known outsourcing site. I got bids from all over the world to work on the design. I ended up going with Ana-Sara, a young woman in Pakistan, who did the job for $100. She was extremely pleasant, professional, accommodating, and despite the time difference, which sometimes left gaps in our email communication, she did a wonderful job. Had I opted to have the blog designed locally in Canada, it would have cost me a minimum of six times what I paid Ana-Sara, maybe even as much as fifteen times, had I gone with a big web company.

> *Imagination is more important than knowledge. For knowledge is limited to all we now know and understand, while imagination embraces the entire world, and all there ever will be to know and understand.*
> **~Albert Einstein~**

As this offshoring of information work continues, the jobs that will be left for North America workers will be conceptual tasks. These jobs require more than basic information processing; they require creativity, a facility with language, and an in-depth knowledge of our culture. These jobs cannot be done as well by a non-native English speaker who does not live in our cultural context. These are the jobs that will remain for North American workers. However, in order to perform these conceptual tasks well, North American workers must have highly developed creative and communicative skills.

Prior to the shift to the "Conceptual Age", it was easy for workers to know how to prepare themselves to enter the workforce. Education used to be the be-all and end-all; if you had a university degree you would be able to find a job, and a good one. That is no longer the case.

A bachelor's degree no longer guarantees young people a good job. Instead of being the mark of a superior education, a university degree is now a minimum requirement for entry into the workforce, much as a high school diploma once was. Canada has the highest rate of tertiary education in the world, with over half of adult Canadians graduating from university. This means that if we have a university degree in Canada, we are merely part of the majority; in order to compete for the best jobs, we need qualifications beyond our degree.

The competition begins even before young people get to university. As more students continue their education beyond graduation from high school, the competition to get into the best universities becomes more heated. In the old world, university admissions committees focused on academic achievement; impressive high school transcripts and high admissions test scores were enough to secure admission to the top schools.

In recent years, however, an emphasis on test performance and a tendency toward grade inflation have resulted in a pool of students whose academic credentials are uniformly stellar. Everyone has good grades, and everyone's admissions test scores are high; admissions committees are forced to look beyond academic achievement in order to identify the best students. When this happens, non-academic achievements become the characteristics that make a student stand out; life experiences, volunteer activities and participation in extracurricular pursuits such as the arts become important. Not coincidentally, these are also the pursuits that will help prepare students to excel in a new, conceptually oriented world.

The global marketplace makes the competitive environment for North American workers even more complicated. Competing with local workers is difficult enough, but young people are no longer competing within the boundaries of their own city or country when they enter the workforce. Fifteen years ago, it did not matter what someone in India was doing, because we did not know about it. It did not affect our job prospects. But the reality of today is very different. We are in competition with workers in India just as surely as we are in competition with someone down the street.

So what does this mean? It means that, if what Daniel Pink says is true (and I think it is), what is required is a completely different approach to teaching our children. We need to teach our children the skills they will need to perform the conceptual creative tasks they will be asked to perform in the global marketplace. If we do not, we are going to have a whole generation of workers who will not be able to compete.

THE APPLE EFFECT

So what are today's employers looking for in prospective employees? They are looking for creative thinkers who can help them position their company in a unique way so that it can compete.

There is no better place to see how this approach to business can work than in the success of *Apple* through the development and marketing of its technology products. Very few companies have been as successful at introducing new products to the marketplace as *Apple*. Their success can be largely attributed to the company's emphasis on its employees' creativity.

Steve Jobs, *Apple's* former CEO, famously rejected the traditional approach to product development, which tends to rely on market research and statistical analyses. Jobs opted instead to encourage his employees to develop products that they liked, having faith that if the company developed products that its own employees liked, the company's customers would like the products, too.

"We didn't build the Mac for anybody else," Jobs said in a 1985 interview. "We built it for ourselves. We were the group of people who were going to judge whether it was great or not. We weren't going to go out and do market research. We just wanted to build the best thing we could build."

Apple's success at selling the products it developed in this way was unprecedented. The success of the *Mac* was followed by the success of the *iPod*, the *iPhone* and the *iPad*. In each case, *Apple* developed products that stayed true to the company's values—making technology that was fun, easy to use and well designed—without being concerned with how the market would react to the products.

The company was doing what ethnographer, Simon Sinek calls sticking with the "why" of what it does—its core values—rather than getting wrapped up in the "what" of its business. It was a process that relied on creativity and innovation, and it worked spectacularly. In effect, *Apple* created the products we wanted before we even knew that we wanted them. Now that is innovation!

But how does *Apple* find creative people? It has learned how to identify them. The company knows that if it does not have creative people on its team, it will not remain a $600 billion company.

"Creativity is just connecting things," Jobs said in a 1996 interview with the magazine, *Wired*. "When you ask creative people how they did something, they feel a little guilty because they didn't really do it, they just saw something. It seemed obvious to them after a while. That's because they were able to connect experiences they've had and synthesize new things. And the reason they were able to do that was that they've had more experiences or they have thought more about their experiences than other people."

Jobs knew that people who are able to stand back and look at things, to see patterns and trends, are the people best equipped to find innovative solutions to problems. Jobs also knew that in the world of traditional business, those people were difficult to find.

"A lot of people in our industry haven't had very diverse experiences," he said. "So they don't have enough dots to connect, and they end up with very linear solutions without a broad perspective on the problem. The broader one's understanding of the human experience, the better design we will have."

The desire to employ creative people is not unique to *Apple*. The most successful companies assemble teams of people who are able to see the big picture, to make connections and to predict market trends. Even in a fiercely competitive job marketplace, these skills will always be in demand. Unfortunately, our traditional systems of education are not designed to produce people with these skills.

THE FAILURE OF EDUCATION

Sir Ken Robinson, author of *Out of Our Minds: Learning to be Creative,* argues that education systems tend to be very linear, and I agree. The path from a problem to its solution, according to this kind of system, progresses through a clear sequence of steps and arrives at the correct answer at the end of that sequence: 2 + 2 = 4, and that's the only right answer.

Most of the time that is how we are taught to learn in school. Unfortunately, the world is not on a linear course. There are rapid changes at every turn, and with the speed at which new technologies are being developed, it is increasingly important that future generations have the skills to bob and weave with the changes and challenges that lie ahead.

As Robinson points out, schools tend to focus on academic achievement, with a strict hierarchy that determines which areas are most important. Math is at the top of the list, and the arts are at the bottom. In particular, as schools are driven to devote their resources to preparing for standardized tests, math becomes a priority, and the arts suffer. In the process, the value of teaching kids to think creatively is significantly diminished.

The problem is that an emphasis on academic learning encourages children to memorize facts and formulae; they are taught to plug the facts into the formula and let the formula spit out the right answer. This is an approach that works well with math, but it does not teach children how to innovate or to come up with ideas that do not conform to the boundaries of the formula.

The limitations of the strictly academic approach will surface later, when students become workers and leaders. When a job calls for innovation or creativity, pure academic achievers—

those students who excel at using formulae, but who have not been encouraged to search for new ideas—are in for a shock. Suddenly, the right answer is not obvious, and they cannot look it up anywhere. Innovative solutions are not produced by a mathematical formula, and a worker who has not learned how to search creatively for new ideas will be unlikely to solve the problem in the best way.

The simple fact is, if we learn mainly in an environment in which we pump out answers that are either right or wrong, with no middle ground and no room for creativity, we will begin to see the whole world in the same way. We will expect every problem to have a right or a wrong answer. If those answers aren't easily derived from the bank of knowledge in our head, the problem seems insurmountable; we see the world in black and white. Participation in the arts, however, opens our mind to the possibility that the world is full of colour, and when we see that colour, we understand that solutions to problems can be found in places where we had never thought to look before.

> **"** *You cannot depend on your eyes when your imagination is out of focus.*
> **~Mark Twain~**

As songwriter Harry Chapin wrote, "There are so many colours in the rainbow," and I feel that a child who has been taught to think creatively will be able to see all of them.

THE IMPORTANCE OF PLAY

If traditional systems of education do not teach our children the skills they will need to excel in the new job market, how then can we make sure that they are learning to be creative, innovative thinkers? One of the ways is through creative play, an activity that children participate in instinctively, but which our education systems methodically discourage us from doing as we grow older. As Robinson points out in his 2006 *TED* Talk, we are born creative, but it is educated out of us.

Children understand the power of imagination to solve problems. Consider the way that a simple cardboard box can be turned by kids into an amazing toy; where adults see only a box, children see an elaborate fort or a spaceship or a fantastic contraption with super powers that can save the world. Children know how to take what they have and look beyond the obvious to find new answers to their questions. The typical four-year-old child is not afraid to try new things or to make wildly innovative suggestions for solving problems.

As we approach adulthood, our ability to solve problems imaginatively is diminished, mostly because the ability is not nurtured and encouraged as we grow older. If we were able to hold on to the ability to actively engage our imaginations, we would be more likely to be successful in those situations that require creative thinking. However, since play is frowned upon for anyone but the youngest children, most of us have lost the sense of wonder and imagination about the world that keeps us thinking creatively.

Unfortunately, once we lose it, it is not easy to get back, especially if our creative skills were not fully developed in the first place. What we can do is try to tap into our child-like spirit of play. In fact, some creative businesses outfit conference rooms with toys, musical instruments and games to encourage employee creativity during brainstorming sessions, but it is never as easy to learn to play as an adult as it was when we were kids.

The benefit of the arts is that young people who participate in artistic pursuits are able to sustain their creative, innovative, and playful urges throughout their lifetime. When involvement in the arts is ongoing, those skills never have a chance to evaporate. Michael Brandwein, an internationally recognized expert in leadership education and author of four best-selling books, connects the lessons we learn during theatre and improvisation training to important leadership skill development. He sees the arts as a way for young people to learn all sorts of valuable life skills, from communication and teamwork skills to intellectual flexibility and self-esteem.

"I would dare somebody to take any of the things you learn from being in a school play or a camp play and *not* apply it to life," Brandwein said during an interview I conducted with him in April of 2012. "Virtually everything in art is tied in some way to what you do."

In our over-programmed world, where children rarely get the chance to come up with their own answers or to step outside the bounds of what everyone else is thinking and doing, they are not developing the creativity they need. The arts give them the opportunity to learn how to be creative and flex their imaginative selves, which ultimately opens more opportunities and avenues of success in their careers when they become adults.

WHAT PARENTS CAN DO

The most important thing parents can do to prepare their children to compete is simply to be aware of the trends. Parents need to realize that old methods of education, those that focus on core subjects at the expense of the arts, are not going to serve their children well in the job market that lies ahead. Parents should be advocates for arts education, and encourage their children to take advantage of creative opportunities.

In Canada, one thing I find challenging is that competition amongst children is often discouraged. Young people are taught that everyone should be equal, and competition is seen as damaging to their self-esteem. This may be an attempt to protect our children or shelter them while they are still young. The problem is, when it comes to being offered opportunities, we are not all equal, and those children who are not able to present themselves well will lose out.

> *Every child is an artist. The problem is how to remain an artist once we grow up.*
> ~Pablo Picasso~

Experiences in the arts can prepare young people for the competitive nature of the world. Even something as basic as auditioning for a school play can help young people get used to the reality that competition is a part of life.

As Michael Brandwein points out, the arts build skills that are important in contexts well beyond performance, skills that will help a child stand out in any field he or she chooses, artistic or not. "Art is a way of learning new things, applying good self-teaching, and it helps you be a good learner," Brandwein says. "When a Mom or a Dad says to me, for example, 'Well, you know, my kid isn't going to be an actor, why be in a play?' This is because you learn things while you're in the play that have nothing to do with making it a career. It has to do with the skills that you have to use and learn in order to have success in the play."

When the play is over, Brandwein knows, the skills remain, and they are the skills young people need not only to survive, but to excel in the twenty-first century.

What can parents do? Enroll their children in arts programming.

CHAPTER FOUR

FEAR IS THE BIGGEST HINDRANCE TO SUCCESS

How Developing Confidence in Children
Opens New Doors

THE FEAR FACTOR

For many people, stage fright is one of their greatest fears. People get physically ill at the thought of speaking in front of their colleagues or making a presentation to clients. Overcoming that fear by consistently confronting the situations that cause us to be afraid is the key to developing confidence that will make us successful in all areas of our life.

Participation in the arts provides just the right kind of fear-defying practice. The skills developed through theatre, for example, not only train us how to deliver a message convincingly, but also build the confidence we need to take command of the stage. As a child, I was very shy, but through consistent practice in improv, I was able to step out of my comfort zone and allow myself to make mistakes. Learning from those mistakes in rehearsal eventually gave me the confidence to perform in front of large audiences.

> *Too many of us are not living our dreams because we are living our fears.*
> **~Les Brown~**

The kind of fear that getting up on stage for the first time evokes is an extreme version of the fear that many—possibly even most—people feel when they are asked to stand up and speak in front of a group. For a performer, the fear is of performing badly, of forgetting lines, of doing something humiliating, of causing an unintended reaction from the audience, of failing. For the public speaker, the fear is very much the same; it is a fear of looking unprepared, of being judged harshly, of saying the wrong things, of failing.

We develop these fears over time, allowing them to become more powerful as we grow older. Most young children have not honed their fear of failure. The typical four-year-old is not afraid to be wrong; he will try anything, and if he is wrong, he will try something else. Just as our creativity is educated out of us, as Sir Ken Robinson explains, our fear of failure is educated into us. The trade-off of creativity for fear does not work in our favour. "If you're not prepared to be wrong," Robinson says, "you'll never come up with anything original."

But how does it happen? How are we trained to be so afraid of failure? I'm going to speak frankly and say that most adults are to blame for the lack of confidence we see in our children. Why? This is because we do not always realize how our words affect others. We tend to tell children more of what we do not like than what we do like. It is not so pleasant being on the receiving end of that, and I am sure you have been there. Think about it; if you are a parent, or teacher or work with children in any capacity, listen to the things you say. "No." "Stop doing that." "You're wrong." The emphasis on failure is unrelenting.

After a while, we come to expect the negativity. We are conditioned to assume bad things over good in our interactions with others. From a young age, children are outfitted with an 'emotional backpack', a burden loaded down with all the negativity they receive from the world around them. They carry that backpack everywhere, and each negative comment—"Can't you do anything right?" "Why are you so clumsy?"—just makes the backpack heavier.

As we fill up our children's backpacks, we feed the insatiable appetite of negativity. The Law of Attraction, that mystical theory that suggests that we get more of whatever we focus on, warns us that emphasizing the negative will only bring more negative experiences into our lives. If our children lack confidence and are overburdened with fear, we can blame ourselves for focusing on what they are doing wrong instead of what they are doing right.

The effect of this negativity is devastating. Young people with a lack of confidence do not want to try new things. They focus on the negativity around them, using it as justification for their own fears. When they do give something a try, they give up easily when the going gets tough. They are uncomfortable in social situations, have trouble making friends, and are reluctant to answer questions in class. They are not, in short, prepared to be successful.

I understand that no one likes to be wrong, but not to try something because of the risk of being wrong limits us in so many ways—grades in school, relationships with others, job opportunities, and so on. It closes off incredible possibilities that are just waiting to come into our lives. Learning from trying and making mistakes is what makes us grow and change, and it is only through change that great things happen.

So how do we bring confidence out in young people? Obviously, we can strive to end the emphasis on negativity; we can let them know when they have done things right. We can also give them confident role models who share their mistakes to show them that being wrong is an essential step toward succeeding. But most of all, we can give them lots of opportunities to succeed. Confidence comes from competence, and competence comes with practice.

MY OWN CONFIDENCE JOURNEY

I vividly remember being about eight years old and going to the convenience store around the corner with my dad to buy *The Sunday New York Times*. It was his guilty pleasure every week. I asked my dad if I could have a chocolate bar. He said yes, but I had to take it up to the counter and give it to the sales clerk, who would then tell me how much money it was. After I had done that, my dad would give me the money, and I would pay the amount.

I almost died. "You want me to do what?" I remember thinking. The thought of having to go up to a complete stranger and pay for a Snickers bar was absolutely horrifying. I told my dad that I could not do it, and I remember begging him to do it for me. He said, "The only way you are getting that chocolate bar is if you pay for it yourself." There was definitely a temper tantrum and some crying in an attempt to sway him, but he refused to back down. I left the store without my treat and a face full of tears.

The funny thing is that I still remember that moment, and I wish I could actually thank my dad for doing that. He passed away ten years ago, and I did not realize what he was trying to teach me until now. He wanted me to practice doing something that required confidence—just stepping a little bit out of my comfort zone to attain a goal. Talk about great parenting!

My mother tells me there were many more chocolate bar freak-outs after that. Now I am fairly certain I did not get the confidence I have now from buying candy bars, but I share this story to illustrate the importance of practice. It should be no surprise that I actually found my confidence through theatre. I was always very shy as a child, but when my sister was about nine years old (and I was twelve), she announced that she was going to take acting lessons so she could be a professional actor. Well, since I was always in competition with her, I had to have that, too. I fought hard with my parents to sign me up for classes, and finally they agreed.

> *An essential aspect of creativity is not being afraid to fail.*
> **~Isaac Newton~**

For the five years that followed, I studied improv with the most amazing teacher, Lisa Seward. In our last year at *Yonge Street Players Theatre School*, the advanced improv class got to perform a show at *The Second City*. We were going to take to the very same stage as comedy legends like Andrea Martin, John Candy, Catherine O'Hara and Eugene Levy. Their names were even etched into the backstage walls! I remember being so pumped and excited and *ready* to perform for a full house. It was an amazing experience.

Would I have been ready to perform at *The Second City* at age twelve on my first day of class? No. I remember barely participating that first day. I was ready because I had practiced. For five years I did improv scenes in a church basement with my fellow actors, and we improved by creating scenes that did not always work. We got constant feedback from our teacher with suggestions of new things to try. So over time, our confidence grew. When a scene went well, we received praise from our audience. We felt great pride from the applause, and the success was extremely motivating.

CONFIDENCE THROUGH THE ARTS

Learning by making mistakes is a skill, and I believe it is very important for young people to hone this skill. In school, almost everything is marked and evaluated. The teacher is always judging the students, and some of them become afraid to try because they do not want to be told they are wrong. The great thing about the arts is that they avoid the traps of judgment; the focus is not on right and wrong answers. When the pressure of needing to find the right answer is removed, it becomes easier to take a risk and try—and trying is the only way to succeed.

Improv-style acting is a fantastic way to practice this kind of risk taking. There are no scripts in improv, so jumping into a scene and just going for it is a huge risk that teaches many valuable lessons. We have no idea if the scene we are creating will make sense, if it will be funny, or if our character choices will resonate with the audience, but we keep trying and putting ourselves out there. If we have a great teacher, she will give us feedback about what we are doing well. Sometimes the scenes will be amazing and sometimes not, but we are encouraged to keep learning from the mistakes.

So what if the scene does not work? Most of the time we are afraid the reactions of others will be far worse than they actually are. Are we laughed at when we make a mistake? Ridiculed? Publicly humiliated? Usually not. But we make the possibility of that happening so real in our heads, it stops us from trying.

Our thoughts have an incredible power over us, so why not start to shift the way we think in a more positive direction? The consistent act of jumping into the unknown of an improv scene and trying something new created a habit of mind that allowed me to keep doing the same thing in other aspects of my life as an adult. There is always the risk that something may not work, but what if it does? We never know unless we try. Taking the risk, raising our hands in class, trying something that is a little scary may just open doors to opportunities we thought only possible in our dreams.

Some of the most successful performers were once shy kids who used the stage to help themselves gain confidence and break through their shyness. Actor Al Pacino, whose on-camera persona is anything but introverted, has admitted to being challenged by his shyness. He says that learning to be comfortable while being the focus of an audience's attention has helped him confront his shyness. "My first language was shy," says Pacino. "It's only by having been thrust into the limelight that I have learned to cope with my shyness."

WHAT IT MEANS FOR THEIR CAREER

I have worked with hundreds of young people over the years, and many of them do not know what they are good at. They have not been told or have never been given the opportunity to discover it. They have been told more often what they are not good at, where they have failed, and where they haven't measured up to expectations.

When young people are given an outlet to develop confidence, it opens up new possibilities they did not know were there. They find their strengths and talents, and they learn how to stretch their capabilities. They come to know themselves; they know what they do well, and they are willing to take important risks because they know the value of taking a chance.

Dr. Katharine Brooks, author of *You Majored in What? Mapping Your Path from Chaos to Career,* agrees that having the right level of confidence is crucial for career success, and she identifies a willingness to take risks—a skill that involvement in the arts surely develops—as a valuable asset for any worker.

"Try something new, even if you're unsure or afraid," she says in a *Forbes* article written by Jacquelyn Smith. "Take baby steps if needed, but begin to immerse yourself in the new project or activity and see how it goes. Try to refrain from judging your performance too early in the process, or comparing your performance to someone who has been doing that activity for a much longer period of time."

Teens who have not been given the opportunity to develop confidence struggle to sell themselves in a job interview because they do not have a strong enough sense of the value of their own abilities and experiences. On the other hand, young people who have done the work—who have spent years putting themselves out there, failing and succeeding and learning from each success or failure—will be sure of themselves and able to project their confidence so that prospective employers can see it. It is those young people who will land the job and they will do it well.

"When someone exudes confidence, we want to work with them," says business consultant William Arruda in the same *Forbes* article. Arruda describes personal branding—having a

> " We are what we repeatedly do. Excellence, therefore, is not an act but a habit.
>
> **~Aristotle~**

strong sense of who you are and communicating that self-image to others—as a key to success in a business career. "We are more likely to follow their lead. Confidence is the number one by-product of the personal branding process, because in branding you uncover what makes you exceptional and use it to make career choices and deliver outstanding value."

WHAT ADULTS CAN DO

In my own development as a camp director, I have read many books about working with children, but one of the most useful approaches I have picked up is from Michael Brandwein in his book, *Super Staff SuperVision*. He says it is easier to identify what we do not like in a child's behaviour than what we do like. The challenge is to be able to identify and describe the good things you see so that you can praise the good behavior and encourage more of it.

> *Anyone who has never made a mistake has never tried anything new.*
> **~Albert Einstein~**

Karen Stephens, author and director of the *Illinois State University Child Care Center* agrees and suggests that parents should emphasize exploration and imagination in their child's play. They should resist perfectionism or negative criticism of their child's creative endeavours, and instead, take an active role in their child's imaginative play.

"Kids get a big boost from parents' getting on the floor and really playing with them," she says. "During play follow your child's lead. Play should be a dance between you, not a concert with you as sole conductor."

Perhaps the most important thing that adults can do to encourage children to have confidence in their creative abilities is to let them know that taking risks and making mistakes is an indispensible part of the creative process. Parents who focus on the learning opportunities of their children's mistakes will help them develop greater levels of confidence. When this happens, possibilities of what they can achieve are significantly increased. Let this be our goal for all children.

CHAPTER FIVE

WHAT DO I DO?

Seeing Problems as Exciting Challenges
Waiting to be Solved

IT'S ALL ABOUT MINDSET

We have all heard the old saying about how to tell an optimist from a pessimist: the optimist looks at half a glass of water and sees it as half full, while the pessimist looks at the same glass and sees one that is half empty. It is a simple way to look at the world, but it reveals an important truth about the power of mindset. The way we choose to see ourselves, the world around us and the challenges we face, determines how we are able to handle the obstacles that cross our paths.

I have spoken about how negativity can undermine our confidence and make us unwilling to take risks. Having a 'half-empty' worldview affects not just our risk-taking abilities, but every aspect of how we deal with the world. A pessimistic outlook hinders our ability to make good decisions, to trust others and to take full advantage of the opportunities that are presented to us. Most importantly, however, having a negative mindset significantly handicaps our ability to solve problems.

Dr. Nido Qubein, a renowned business consultant, author and motivational speaker who has given more than 5,000 presentations since 1974, suggests that the ability to solve problems determines what we are able to attain from life. Life does not offer what we need, Qubein says, it offers what we deserve, and if we want to deserve more, we have to become more valuable. Our value, he says, is directly determined by the size of the problems we are able to solve. If we want to be more valuable, we have to be able to solve bigger problems. The best problem-solvers, Qubein argues, are those who focus on results rather than obstacles. They are, in other words, the people with a positive mindset.

All of us are going to encounter problems; they are an un-avoidable part of life. However, the key to navigating success-fully past a problem is to resist seeing it as an impenetrable brick wall. If we give up as soon as we come up against a problem, we will never accomplish anything. Consider inventors like the Wright brothers, the famous pioneers of flight; they achieved a successful flight of their powered aircraft in 1903 after four years of trial and error, during which, design after design failed to perform the way the brothers hoped it would. If the Wright brothers had given in to the problems they encountered, the development of some of the world's most important technology would have been delayed for who knows how long.

Think about a time in your own life when you had a prob-lem. Did you try everything you could to solve the problem before you gave up, or did you give up the second it became difficult? Be honest with yourself. If you are like most of us, you stopped trying before you ex-hausted every possibility for find-ing a solution. Why do we do this? Why are we so willing to quit when the going gets tough?

John Assaraf, who calls him-self the "Spiritual Entrepreneur," says that we quit because we set ourselves up to be quitters, often without even realizing we are doing it.

> " You can never solve a problem on the level on which it was created.
> **~Albert Einstein~**

"Often we go through the day giving ourselves all sorts of contradictory, or even negative messages," Assaraf says. "We may project confidence to the world around us, while our inner dialogue says, 'I hope this works. I am so nervous about this. I hope I don't blow it.' Affirmations are self-fulfilling prophecies. If we say, 'This is never going to work,' then chances are excellent, it never will."

We tell ourselves these negative things because we have been taught that it is the way to approach problems. Very early on, we learn from adult role models what is possible and what is not. For example, a child might say, "I want to learn guitar." A parent might respond, "You can't even get your homework done, how are you going to learn guitar?" Unfortunately, many children grow up in environments that stifle possibilities. As Ken Robinson explains, children have the right mindset, but adults are teaching them to give up by example and with discouraging words. By doing this adults are limiting what is possible for children.

BEFORE QUITTING IS AN OPTION

So why do we equate problem-solving with difficulty? It is not a natural mindset. Think about young children; a baby has to figure out how to crawl, walk, eat solid foods, talk and dozens of other essential skills. None of them are easy to learn, but a baby never gives up.

As we saw in the previous chapter, young children are not inhibited by the fear of failure. When they are confronted with a new question, they are eager to give an answer. It is only as they grow older that they are trained to be afraid to offer something new. This inhibition comes from years of negativity—"Not again!" "Why don't you ever listen?" "You're wrong."—delivered to children by their teachers and the adults around them. They stop trying because they do not want to be wrong, and they are told over and over again how often they are wrong. Problem-solving becomes wrapped in fear, negativity, failure and inadequacy. It is no wonder that eventually they want to quit at the first hint of a problem.

It does not have to be that way. If the negativity is taken out of the equation, problems are simply what young children know them to be: opportunities to be creative. If young people are used to seeing problems as creative challenges, they will not be discouraged when problems arise. Instead, they will be energized by the challenges and will be eager to jump in and find a solution.

Research highlighted by Fergus Hughes has shown that children who approach problems through play are more successful at finding solutions than children who are faced with a problem in a serious, traditional way. Studies conducted in the 1970s and 1980s concluded that creative play helps children with convergent problem-solving—that is, bringing isolated pieces of information together to achieve a solution. Even more significantly, the studies showed that children who engaged in play while problem-solving were more motivated to solve the problem and were more persistent in finding a solution. In other words, they were not quick to give up.

> ❝ *Inside of every problem lies an opportunity.*
> **~Robert Kiyosaki~**

Therefore, engaging in playful, creative, problem-solving produces motivated, persistent, successful problem-solvers. There is no better way to develop creative problem-solving abilities than through involvement with the arts.

In their book, *Complexity and Education*, Brent Davis and Dennis Sumara describe an important concept in arts education called "enabling constraints". This concept explains that giving an assignment with certain challenging parameters actually promotes creativity. For example, if you say to a group of kids, you have to create a piece of music that represents the life cycle of a butterfly using only percussion instruments, they will immediately start to think of ways they can convey concepts. If you ask them to create a music piece without this constraint, they may actually have writer's block—it is too open. There is nothing to force them to be creative.

In the arts, a problem or constraint is seen as an exciting challenge that stimulates creativity. The point is, the way we look at a problem defines our ability to solve it. If children are in the habit of seeing problems in this positive way, there is nothing life can throw at them that will make them give up. They will be excited by a problem rather than discouraged by it.

THE ART OF PROBLEM-SOLVING

Convincing people of the importance of an education in the arts can be a tough sell. In 2012, core subjects like math and science are heralded above all else, and the general public still tends to overlook the arts. Often when a school faces budget cuts, music, visual art and drama are typically the first to go.

The reality is that we are doing our children a great disservice by not immersing them in the arts. Increasingly, studies are proving how children exposed to an arts curriculum demonstrate increased skills in critical thinking when compared to their peers.

Think about it. Why wouldn't an arts education, with its focus on creativity, produce young people capable of thinking outside the box? Artists are constantly pushed to explore uncharted territory. The truly great ones are those that produce new and exciting work that has never before been created.

A study conducted by the *Guggenheim Museum* showed that a child with an arts background has a considerable advantage over her peers. Entitled, *The Art of Problem Solving*, this four-year research initiative was conducted between 2006 and 2010 and evaluated the impact of the educational program, *Learning Through Art.*

The study showed that children from the *Learning Through Art* program demonstrated stronger problem-solving skills in three out of six areas including, "flexibility, resource recognition, and connection of ends and aims." They found that problem-solving was incorporated into the students' daily art lessons. Students were encouraged to make conscious choices and find multiple answers to any given problem through the creative process.

Artistic creations themselves are born through the solving of problems. Generally, the 'problem' is how to communicate a certain emotion or idea. To create something original, you must first identify the problem, break it down, and then develop different ways to approach and learn from it. For example:

- When an artist holds a lump of clay, she must work within the constraints of the material to figure out how to mold it into a particular form.
- When two dancers work together, they must problem-solve to figure out how to make a particular partnering section work in the choreography.
- When a writer comes up with a story, he must use critical thinking to develop the story and make it clear and exciting for his readers.

- When an actress has a monologue to perform, she must consider how she will express a certain emotion through her voice and body language.

Each artistic endeavor faces some form of challenge in its creation that needs to be overcome. Without even realizing it, young people who participate in the arts are consistently being challenged to solve problems. That same inventive drive is exactly the skill needed to succeed in the realm of technology and innovation.

So, how can conventional education, with its focus on standardized tests, provide students with the same skill development? The answer is, it cannot. I do not mean that schools do not provide opportunities for children to explore their creativity. The problem is, for the majority of the time, students in school are encouraged to come up with one answer—the right one. Young people are not being given enough practice developing problem-solving skills. As a result, young adults are entering the workforce with underdeveloped problem-solving skills.

> " Believe you can and you're halfway there.
> ~Theodore Roosevelt~

Experience in the arts, is therefore not merely desirable, but essential for our children's future success. The arts are building blocks for developing critical thinking in young people so that problems become exciting challenges to be solved, instead of insurmountable roadblocks. Clearly, the arts benefit more than just those young people pursuing a career as a musician, dancer, actor or artist.

Einstein himself said, "Imagination is more important than knowledge. For knowledge is limited to all we now know and understand, while imagination embraces the entire world, and all there ever will be to know and understand."

6 THINGS ADULTS INADVERTENTLY DO TO DISCOURAGE THE DEVELOPMENT OF PROBLEM-SOLVING SKILLS

Let me preface this list by saying that not all adults do these things. However, I think it is fair to say that a large majority of adults do at least one or two of these things on a regular basis. That being said, it is not our fault. As I have discussed, we are conditioned from a young age to focus on the negative. Therefore, we sometimes unknowingly interact with children in a way that perpetuates a negative mindset and prevents them from developing solid problem-solving techniques. It is a cyclical habit, and the only way to break it is to start to become aware of our words and actions and the impact they have on our children.

1. **Giving children the right answer instead of letting them discover it for themselves**

   For example, if adults do homework for their children, they do not learn how to find the answer themselves. Giving the answer to a problem instead of making her discover it for herself does nothing to encourage the development of her problem-solving skills.

2. **Discouraging possibilities**

   Setting limits on possibilities simply perpetuates the glass-half-empty mindset; it teaches children to look for obstacles and barriers rather than solutions, and it severely limits their problem-solving abilities.

3. Lack of patience/persistence

Most problems are not solved quickly or on the first attempt. Adults who have internalized the notion that quitting is an option are likely to model that behaviour for children. They give the child negative problem-solving behaviour to emulate.

4. Being afraid to ask for help

Fear of asking for help is linked with the overall fear of failure. However, knowing when and how to ask for help is an important part of creative problem-solving. Solving a problem means using the right resources to find a solution and often the right resource is help from someone else.

5. Not asking enough questions

The key to teaching problem-solving skills is what Michael Brandwein refers to as "Awareness of Process (AOP)." He has three AOP questions he uses when teaching skills related to leadership: What worked? What didn't? What are you going to do next time? Asking questions is the key to teaching young people how to solve problems.

6. Poor modeling

The fact is that most adults do not have well-developed problem-solving skills, so they are in no position to show children how to go about solving a problem creatively. They are much more likely to model the negative behaviours than to give children a solid example of innovative problem-solving to follow.

For our children to become the best problem-solvers they can be, we need to encourage them to see problems as opportunities, not as obstacles. We need to let them approach problems playfully and with a mindset of optimism. Young children know how to do this but lose the skill over time. Arts training will restore this capability.

Wouldn't it be a wonderful addition to our curriculum to have a class on positive mindset in school? After all, how are young people supposed to view challenges in life as exciting and worthwhile opportunities to learn, if they are not taught to think that way?

CHAPTER SIX

ANYTHING IS POSSIBLE!

How Teaching Kids to Dream Big
Can Change the World

You Never Know

You never know when someone
May catch a dream from you,
You never know when a little word
Or something you might do
May open up the window
Of a mind that seeks the light,
The way you live may not matter at all
But you never know—it might.
And just in case it could be
That another's life, through you,
Might possibly change for the better,
With a broader and brighter view,
It seems it might be worth a try
At pointing the way to what's right,
Of course, it may not matter at all,
But then again—it might.

~author unknown~

I first heard this poem seven years ago at a provincial camp conference. It was read in a large banquet hall in front of several hundred camp directors by Mike Pearse, one of the owners of *Camp Tawingo*. I had never met Mike, but in that moment I knew that I needed to, for anyone who could recite words that would resonate with me so strongly was definitely someone I wanted to get to know. So I did. Mike, along with his wife Tia, became important mentors in my journey as a camp director, and now, after countless interactions, I have pinpointed three important lessons that I have learned from them:

✔ **ONE:** Always see the potential in young people and do whatever you can to foster it.

✔ **TWO:** Material successes in life are nice, but what matters is making a difference in the life of a child.

✔ **THREE:** Encourage the dreams of others, as you never know the impact it may bring.

Mike and Tia always encouraged me to follow my own dreams, and after many years of mentorship and friendship, the consistency of their message has given me enhanced leadership tools that I have been able to pass along to the children and staff I engage with each summer. Each summer I read the *You Never Know* poem to my staff as a reminder of the incredible power we have as adults to impact a child's life.

A simple word of encouragement, or even saying "I'm proud of you" can have a profound effect on the choices a child makes as they grow older. As adults, we can all think back to that one person during our childhood who said or did something that altered our choices, led us down a different path, or opened a door to possibilities we didn't know were there. If you didn't experience such a person, you have the special opportunity to do that for someone in your life right now. For in doing so, you could be awakening someone who is meant to contribute great things to the world.

Maybe a child you know right now is destined for greatness, and all they need is a push to realize their full potential. How do

> ❝ *Do not follow where the path may lead. Go instead where there is no path and leave a trail.*
> **~Ralph Waldo Emerson~**

you know that you haven't met the next Michael Jackson? Or Pablo Picasso? Or George Lucas?

WHEN DREAMS FADE BEFORE THEY ARE MEANT TO...

As someone who has worked with young people for over sixteen years, I can honestly say that one of the greatest gifts I have instilled in them is the idea that anything is possible. I know I have taught them many other valuable skills and life-lessons, but for me, that one is the most meaningful. I believe children are born with boundless potential. They are open vessels into which knowledge can be poured and creativity fostered, but somewhere along the way, they also learn to be fearful and start doubting their own potential.

For some kids, that fear and doubt is reinforced by others around them, whether it be peers at school, a family member or a total stranger. It is for those kids, that my heart cries, because I have seen what happens to a child whose wonder about the world has been stifled. They give up on themselves.

Throughout my career as an arts educator and camp director I have worked with many children who were on the path to giving up. Maybe they weren't strong academically or they had trouble making friends and got bullied because of it. Maybe they were surrounded by too many negative influences in their community and did not have the strength or guidance from a positive role model to see other possibilities in their life. Or perhaps the adults in their life were working at high-powered jobs and just did not have the time to spend nurturing their abilities.

One thing I have realized is that when a child has begun the downward spiral into hopelessness, it takes something big to reignite their ability to dream. So how do we do that?

Here is the big secret...

**Kids need to feel a significant sense of achievement
and be acknowledged for it.**

It is simple, and engaging in the arts is one of the best ways I have seen to achieve this.

Participation in the arts gives young people the opportunity to challenge themselves and receive a positive response at the same time. When these experiences are combined it does wonders to reinvigorate a child's faith in the power of dreams. Getting up on a stage for the first time is a huge step for most kids, and when they do it, they see immediately that they are capable of pushing beyond the limits of what they thought they could do. As they continue to work on their performance skills, particularly when they are part of an ensemble, they learn that they are important, that they are part of a team and others are relying on them to help bring an artistic creation to life. When they take their final bow, the applause from the audience is a gesture of recognition and appreciation that is a powerful affirmation that the dream was worth pursuing.

When the arts help a child to dream, they do not just improve his present reality, they make his future brighter, too. A United States *National Endowment for the Arts* report released in March 2012 showed that among at-risk students, more than twice as many kids with involvement in the arts planned to pursue a professional career (law, medicine, education or management) as those who had no experience with the arts. Arts-involved young people get better grades, have higher rates of college enrollment, and are more likely to volunteer in their communities, vote and become involved in local politics. They are, in short, more optimistic about what is ahead of them, and they are more likely to set and achieve goals.

The list of studies and data that support the importance of the arts goes on and on. In Canada, a National Study that assessed the *Royal Conservatory of Music's Learning Through the Arts* program showed that there is a clear correlation between improved student performance in mathematics, language, and involvement in the arts. Just as in the American study, the Canadian study concluded that participation in the arts elevated students' attitude toward academics overall.

These recent studies can be added to the multitude of studies in the 1990s, which indicated that the arts help children to develop imagination, self-esteem and a motivation to learn. To put it simply, the data shows that the arts make kids' lives better, and as Mike and Tia's second lesson made clear to me, there is nothing more important than that.

BECAUSE OF TRISTAN I KNEW THEY WERE LISTENING

For years I consciously, and sometimes unconsciously, seized opportunities to spark dreams within the children I worked with. In 2010, an incredible thing happened. I finally received confirmation that they had been listening to me. I finally received recognition that my sometimes over-enthusiastic zest for life had made an impact and not fallen on deaf ears.

We were on a weekend overnight trip at Camp Tawingo and wrapping up a leadership session with our oldest campers. Mike Pearse, who was facilitating the session, posed the final questions to the group, "What have you learned from your experiences at arts camp?" "What is the one thing that you will carry with you?"

Many of the teens who raised their hands spoke about a specific artistic skill they learned that made them feel more advanced or prepared for school. Others spoke about the sense of community and belonging they felt by being surrounded by like-minded people. Then a boy named Tristan raised his hand and said, "I guess I learned it from Lisa, that anything is possible. You can do anything you want in life. If I want to be a famous basketball player or a recording artist I can be. She followed her dream and made this camp for all of us, so I can too."

> *There are those who look at things the way they are, and ask why. I dream of things that never were, and ask why not?*
> **~Robert Kennedy~**

I was sitting at the back of the room, and all eyes shifted in my direction to see my reaction. I could especially feel the eyes of the staff in the room waiting for my response. I must admit, I did start to tear up a bit, but it is not because I am an overly emotional person. It was because Tristan was the one who said it. Tristan had been a camper of mine for five years, and to say he had a rocky start would be an understatement. He went from throwing chairs when he was angry to being one of the most positive and strongest leaders in camp. I realize this is an extreme example, but I share this story because it was an 'aha' moment for me. There was Mike and Tia's third lesson—encourage the dreams of others because you never know the impact it will have. Right there before my eyes, Tristan's comment showed me that all we need to do is teach children how to dream big, and why it matters in their life.

LEARNING TO DREAM BIG!

Whether it is financial success on Bay Street (Wall Street if you are American) or discovering a cure for cancer, one needs to learn how to dream big in order for incredible things to happen. As I mentioned in chapter four, my theatre troupe when I was a teenager had an improv show at *The Second City*. I recall being struck by the fact that John Candy and Catherine O'Hara stood on the same stage that I stood on and launched incredible careers. After that night, my fellow cast members and I spent hours writing scripts we planned to pitch to Lorne Michaels for *Saturday Night Live (SNL)*. At age fifteen, our success on stage taught us to believe our dreams were possible. Okay, so I am not a scriptwriter for *SNL*, but when I decided to start my own arts organization I was not afraid, despite the fact that people were warning me that it would be extremely difficult.

Young people have a unique opportunity to learn how to dream big through participating in the arts. Whether it is putting on a show to perform in front of an audience in only four weeks or creating a mural to display in a public park, the arts teach kids how to have an idea and see it through to fruition. The arts teach them to push beyond the boundaries of what they think they are capable of achieving. As adults, it is our responsibility to foster the dreams of young people, no matter how big or challenging those dreams may be to achieve.

> " *Our truest life is when we are in dreams awake.*
> **~Henry David Thoreau~**

"I am the product of my parents encouraging me to draw, my teachers encouraging me to draw, my librarian encouraging me," says Tony DiTerlizzi, co-author and illustrator of the best-selling *Spiderwick Chronicles* books during a *PBS* interview. "All the adults who were in my life encouraged me to draw and to keep doing it, to keep my head in the clouds and keep coming up with stories. All the adults in my life, when I was a little kid, kept encouraging me. That's why I'm here today."

I have read many inspirational words that have since motivated me in my work and have pushed me to take my artistic skills to new heights. I am fortunate to have been surrounded by family and friends who have encouraged my dreams, no matter how difficult they may be to achieve. When we are little, we believe we can be anything we want. "Mommy, I want to be a rocket scientist!" "Daddy, I want to be a famous pop star!" Often the response is "You can be anything you want to be." Sadly, somewhere along the way that notion changes.

THE REALITY BALANCE

As kids get older and become adolescents, the idea of achieving great things by following their dreams gets stuck in what many adults call 'reality'. "It's too competitive." "You aren't good enough." "There is no security in that kind of career." Many adults have this nasty little habit of restricting the dreams of those around them because of their own fear of failure. With all due respect, if that is your attitude, please keep it to yourself. Anybody who has contributed something of significance to the world usually did so because they had an idea or a dream and had the guts to follow it and not give up.

"When you crush a child's dream, you're crushing the child," says author and nationally respected career counselor Robin Ryan in a 2004 article in *The Buffalo News*. "If you want your child to be happy, she's not going to enjoy becoming a lawyer if she really wants to be an artist."

Parents often fall into the trap of thinking that if they encourage their children to dream, they are setting the kids up for disappointment when they ultimately fail. It is true that the world is a difficult place, and our children will not be successful in everything they attempt, but encouraging them to dream and to pursue their dreams allows us to teach the parallel lessons of perseverance and dedication. Our children will not achieve their dreams just because they have one; they will achieve their dreams because they never lose sight of those dreams, and they never stop working toward them.

There is no question that a balance must be struck between dreaming big and understanding that pursuing a dream is hard work. Dreams do not become reality without effort on the part of the dreamer; work ethic is an essential element in the story of just about every achieved dream. Young people sometimes look at a career in the arts and see the glamour and fun of performing, and they overlook the long hours of hard work and unwavering attention that make artists successful. The arts sometimes look easy, when nothing could be further from the truth.

However, there is a fine line between making sure that young people remember the hard work that dreams require and discouraging the dream. Parents need to encourage realistically, but they still need to encourage. There is room for both dreams and work ethic in the minds of our children, and we need to make sure they know that. We should all remember Mike and Tia's first lesson;

we need to see the potential in our young dreamers, and we need to see it as our responsibility to keep their dreams alive.

KEEP DREAMING AND CHANGE THE WORLD

In the last chapter, I used the Wright brothers as an example of inventors who resisted the urge to quit when their initial inventions failed, but let's not forget that the Wright brothers had to deal with external discouragement, too. Before the brothers flew, critics openly and loudly claimed that they would never be able to achieve powered flight, calling them "bluffers" and frauds. They had a dream and they remained focused on it until it became reality.

Consider the example of world-changing innovation we looked at in chapter three: Steve Jobs and *Apple.* Jobs and his partner, Steve Wozniak established *Apple* in a garage because they had a dream of making a new kind of computer. Their goal was to take on corporate giants like *IBM*, a company that at the time seemed immune to competitive challenges from even the biggest technology corporations, let alone a tiny start-up. All the voices of wisdom told Jobs that his dream had no hope of coming true. Not much more than three decades later, Jobs' dream has turned into one of the most valuable companies in the world, and *Apple's* products have changed the way that millions of people communicate. If Jobs had listened to all the people who, in the 1970s,

> ❝ *Twenty years from now you will be more disappointed by the things that you didn't do than by the ones you did do.*
> **~Mark Twain~**

said that his dream was crazy, none of this would have happened.

Where would Craig Kielburger be today had his dream of helping impoverished children around the world been stifled? When Craig was twelve years old, he read a story in the *Toronto Star* about a twelve-year-old Pakistani factory worker who had been murdered for speaking out against the practice of child labour. Craig and a group of his classmates established an organization with the goal of increasing awareness of the child labour problem. By 2010, fifteen years after its foundation, the organization, *Free The Children*, had raised money to build 650 schools, which educate 55,000 children a day.

If Craig had been told that he should face 'reality' when he first had his dream, *Free The Children* would not exist, and what a sad thing that would be. Craig's organization has impacted more than one million young people in forty-five countries around the world, all because at the age of twelve, Craig had a dream and followed it.

So the next time you have the opportunity to inspire someone to dream, whether they are a child or an adult, please do it! Because you never know when someone may catch a dream from you and change the world forever.

CHAPTER SEVEN

IT'S ALL ABOUT ACCOUNTABILITY

How the Arts Foster Relationship
Building Skills Needed for Success

Sadly, taking responsibility is an important skill that many of us lack. There are two reasons for this. First, it is difficult to take responsibility for our actions, especially mistakes. There is a common misconception in our society that making a mistake is a character flaw. This misconception, coupled with a fear of failure, is enough to paralyze anyone. People unfortunately equate making a mistake with failing as a human being. Everyone makes mistakes. As Alexander Pope famously said, "To err is human." It is what we do after we make a mistake that demonstrates our strength of character.

In the world of business, some CEOs are seeing failures as a positive thing—a way to gain new insights about their customers and what will ultimately determine market success. "Figuring out how to master this process of failing fast and failing cheap and fumbling toward success is probably the most important thing companies have to get good at," says Scott Anthony of the consulting firm *Innosight* in a 2006 article in *Bloomberg Business Week Magazine*. Failing well—without huge profit losses—is something that companies strive to do. It encourages learning about what is working and what aspects of a business need to be refined. If children are taught to value mistakes and learn from them when they are young, they will be excellent at identifying these learning opportunities when they are in leadership positions in the workforce.

This leads to the second reason many of us are not willing to take responsibility for our actions. Those who refuse to take the blame when they make a mistake, either want to avoid taking responsibility for the real consequences, or they have an underdeveloped sense of empathy. Accountability is rooted in the connection between our actions and our empathy for other people. We feel accountable when we understand how our actions affect others, but in order to understand this, we have to be able to imagine how other people feel. We need to be able to put ourselves in the other person's place and feel what he is feeling. We need to be able to step outside of what we want, and think about how our actions are perceived by and affect others.

ACCOUNTABILITY & RELATIONSHIPS

We do not achieve in isolation. No matter how much we wish we could be entirely independent, we need others to help us along the way, to guide us, to support us, and to help us accomplish the things that we need to do. Our success in life depends in large part on the relationships we have with other people—family, friends and business associates. It is through healthy relationships with all these people that we are able to achieve this success.

> " While we are free to choose our actions, we are not free to choose the consequences of our actions.
> ~Stephen R. Covey~

Unfortunately, too many of us are losing the ability to forge the right kind of bonds with those around us because we are not treating them the way they should be treated.

An important part of building healthy relationships is being able to ask for help. Unfortunately this is still seen as a sign of weakness. Many people are afraid to ask for help because they think they will be seen as dependent, weak, and not able to cope. Asking for help is actually a sign of strength. It shows the person we are asking that we are willing to admit we are not perfect. We are human. It also shows them our goal is personal development. We are always willing to learn.

We have all worked with someone who refuses to take responsibility for his own actions. Nothing that goes wrong is ever their fault, and it is never their responsibility to come up with any solution. No one wants to work with someone like that. Why? This is because ultimately it means the blame shifts to others and the responsibility of dealing with the consequences shifts with it. When people sidestep accountability and try to remain free of responsibility, others see them as unreliable and untrustworthy. Avoiding accountability is no way to build healthy relationships, and it is not the pathway to a successful life and career.

Accountability demonstrates strength of character. Our ability to accept accountability tells the world who we are. People will have respect for us if they can see that we are willing to own up to the part we play in any given situation.

MY OWN ACCOUNTABILITY CONFESSION

My own development of these skills truly started to develop at a more advanced level in my mid-twenties. In my first year as a camp director, I was twenty-six years old. I was now the boss and responsible for everything that went on at the arts camp I was running. I always took that responsibility extremely seriously. However, it was not always easy to be accountable for mistakes or accept responsibility for my own shortcomings. I was far from perfect, but I think that was harder to take ownership of when I was younger. I have to admit there were a few instances when I did pass the blame onto others or bend the truth a little to avoid being seen in a negative light. It is easy for me to admit that now, because I can see such a shift in my own skill level when it comes to accountability. I look back at the twenty-six year old version of myself and smile and think…wow did you have a lot to learn!

So I did! Over the years, I started to read books on leadership, participate in workshops and learn through coaching from experts in the field. I started to see my role as a director not as being at the top of a hierarchical pyramid of who was most important, but at the bottom. As the director, I had to lay the foundation for everything that happened at camp. I had to support every role, whether it was a first year junior counsellor or an experienced theatre instructor. As the years went on and I enhanced my own leadership skills, I recognized that I had to set what the culture of the organization would be like and taking accountability was a big part of that. When I started to take more accountability for my choices and actions, I found that I forged stronger relationships with my staff and in turn developed a much stronger team.

ACCOUNTABILITY AND EDUCATION

In a 2005 article in the journal *College Teaching,* instructors Holly Hassel and Jessica Lourey argued that a lack of personal accountability among college students was reaching dire proportions. "More than ever," they wrote, "students expect to be catered to, to receive a B or better for merely paying for the class and making a good faith effort."

Students, in other words, fail to see a connection between the way they perform in class and the grade they receive for the class. They have lost sight of their own responsibility for their academic success. They believe success is something owed to them, something that should come to them automatically. They do not realize it has to do with how hard they work and how they behave.

"More than ever," Hassel and Lourey wrote, "college instructors have reason to believe that their students are out of touch with what their grades really symbolize, why they are even in college, and what responsibilities they have as students."

There are a variety of reasons for this lack of personal accountability. Some students are apathetic about their education, and that apathy often leads to absenteeism and poor performance. However, perhaps the most significant contributing factor to the decline in accountability is grade inflation. High school and university students are getting higher grades than they did in the past for the same work. If students are able to get a high grade without putting in much effort, why would they try harder? It makes sense that they would start to lose touch with the connection between what they do (or do not do) and their grades.

Experts say that there is a combination of factors that contribute to grade inflation, including political pressure for schools to have the highest GPAs and pressure on teachers from parents and students. In a 2001 article in *The Chicago Maroon*, Harvey Mansfield, a professor of government at *Harvard University* suggests that another contributing factor is North America's obsession with increasing children's self-esteem. "According to that therapeutic notion, the purpose of education is to make students feel capable and empowered. So to grade them, or to grade them strictly, is cruel and dehumanizing," Mansfield said. "No longer is the job of a professor a sort of taskmaster, but rather to be a friend, always patting you on the back."

From my perspective, fostering a strong sense of self-esteem is extremely important, but it does not mean we should not hold children to high standards. Making a child feel good about themselves should not come at the expense of teaching them the values of hard work and perseverance.

This lack of accountability is not only happening in the classroom. As I mentioned in the first chapter, we are becoming less willing to hold young people accountable for their actions because we do not want them to feel stressed. 'Helicopter' parents, in particular, think they are de-stressing their children by allowing them to avoid taking responsibility. Unfortunately, these parents are doing the opposite.

When I was a child, I was enrolled in piano lessons, but like many others, did not practice regularly. My mother warned me on several occasions that if I did not start practicing, the lessons would be taken away. Unfortunately, I failed to find the discipline to practice and my mother followed through on her promise. Despite my protests, she did not give in. Thus, I remain at a grade three piano level, but I did learn that my actions have consequences.

When there is no accountability, there is no reason to believe that our actions really matter. If we want our children to be successful in navigating the adult world, we need to focus less on protecting them and more on giving them opportunities to step up and take responsibility for their actions.

ACCOUNTABILITY IN THE GLOBAL ERA

In 2012, a video of a sixty-eight year old school bus monitor being relentlessly bullied by a group of four young boys gained notoriety online. It was a clear example of a lack of accountability; these adolescent boys were willing to behave viciously and cruelly because they believed they would not be held responsible for their actions. It is also an example of how current technology and the interconnectedness of our world is capable of bringing about a return of accountability.

When the video of the bus bullying was posted online, it quickly went viral, and when the cruelty of the boys' behaviour was seen around the world, both support for the victim and condemnation of the boys was universal. The bullies received death threats, a year's suspension from school and a requirement to perform community service with senior citizens. It was a harsh lesson, but no harsher than the behaviour that inspired it; the boys were being held accountable.

> *It is wrong and immoral to seek to escape the consequences of one's acts."*
> **~Mahatma Gandhi~**

The lesson to be learned is that we never know when something we do is going to be noticed and have consequences beyond what we thought. If the kids involved in these incidents had learned responsibility for their actions early on, they would have thought twice about doing what they did. Instead, they assumed that their choices would have no consequences, and they were proven wrong in a very harsh, global way. It was the world calling them out on their actions.

IT'S NOT MY FAULT

When we see someone in his/her early twenties dodging accountability, it shows a lack of maturity. It shows that he/she is not ready to improve or learn from feedback.

We cannot lay all the blame on the young people. Our expectations of them, or our lack of expectations, are what determine how responsible they will be. We set the tone, and they follow. "It's grownups, not teenagers, who have honed the values, expectations and opportunities from which our nation's youth develop their work habits," writes Erika Christakis in a *Time* magazine article. "If we want a more respectful and industrious workforce, we need to do a better job creating one."

Part of the problem is that kids are not gaining life experiences that build accountability and a sense of responsibility. "It was once common to see teenagers mowing lawns, waiting tables, digging ditches and bagging groceries for modest wages in the long summer months," writes Christakis. "Summer employment was a social equalizer, allowing both affluent and financially strapped teenagers to gain a foothold on adulthood, learning the virtues of hard work, respect and teamwork in a relatively low-stakes atmosphere. But youth employment has declined precipitously over the years, and young people are losing a chance to develop these important life skills in the process."

ACCOUNTABILITY AND THE ARTS

So how do we do it? How do we create a generation of young people who are responsible and accountable, who can be successful in their careers and in life, and who can move the world forward? One way that we can do it is to teach children accountability through involvement in the arts.

The arts can help to build accountability in a number of different ways. Firstly, training in the arts helps children to develop their empathy for others. As I explained earlier in this chapter, empathy is the key to connecting our behaviour with the effect of our actions. Secondly, the arts also encourage young people to overcome their fear of failure and, consequently, their fear of the consequences of their failures. Once they have overcome that fear, they will be more willing to take responsibility for their actions.

Building Empathy through the Arts

One of the most direct and obvious connections between the arts and empathy lies in theatre education. Clearly, immersing ourselves in a character is an exercise in learning to understand how someone else feels. As we examine the intentions and motivations of the character we are playing, we are putting ourselves inside that character's head and learning to see through eyes that are not our own. Beyond that, we will think about how other characters are going to react to our character, and will eventually develop the ability to empathize with a wide range of individuals.

Sometimes it is the introspection required by creativity that makes empathy blossom. A 2011 article in *The Wall Street Journal* describes a number of medical school programs that use the arts to encourage new doctors to treat their patients with empathy. "I think if you write a lot of reflective pieces or emotionally charged pieces you do become more in tune with other people," explains one medical student who participated in one of the programs. "When I wrote a reflection on a patient I didn't really like, putting it down on paper made me start to see things from their perspective." I have heard of many other professional development programs that help adults develop empathy. My question is, why are so many people growing up without this invaluable skill in the first place?

Similar to joining a sports team, simply being part of a dance or music ensemble breeds empathy and fosters accountability. Along with everyone else in the ensemble, you are part of a team. Everyone contributes to the success of the music or dance piece. You have to show up on time and be prepared, or the whole group suffers. You have to be there for rehearsals, and you have to practice your part on your own; you are part of a greater whole, and if you do not do what is expected of you—if you miss rehearsals or you do not know your part—you are going to let the other members of the ensemble down. Everyone depends on you the same way that you depend on everyone else; it is a crash course in empathy.

Overcoming Fear Through Critique

One major obstacle to fostering a spirit of accountability is the fear of failure I discussed in chapter four. When we are afraid to fail, we are eager to avoid responsibility. If we are never to blame for anything, we can never be wrong, and we can never fail. As teachers, the best thing we can do for students is to let them know that it is acceptable to fail and that, in fact, sometimes success comes directly from failure. "Each time you fail," says painter Fernando Gerassi, "you learn something. If you have faith in yourself you accept the failure and go on. The more failures the better." Once we are able to remove the fear of failure, accountability is not such a scary thing either.

With an intentional approach to learning in the arts, teachers will set up an environment where critique is a constant part of the learning process. This helps children to understand that feedback should not be taken personally, but that it is meant to challenge them to push beyond what they think they are capable of achieving. A good art teacher's critique is specific; it tells the student what works, what does not and what they can do to improve.

> *He that is good for making excuses is seldom good for anything else.*
>
> ~Benjamin Franklin~

This cultivates an attitude that learning is never done and to achieve success, they must persist. Training in the arts teaches the mindset that through self-observation and accepting feedback from others, mistakes are not the end of the world; they are part of the learning process.

Being able to accept feedback, allows us to develop the skill of accountability. If we have been used to seeing feedback as fuel for improvement, our natural reaction when receiving feedback at work will not be to make excuses, but to ask for more feedback about how we can improve our performance. How impressed will our boss be?

ACCOUNTABILITY FOR FUTURE SUCCESS

An employee who has a willingness to learn from feedback, a clear sense of responsibility, and a sincere empathy for others is the employee who is most likely to succeed. He will be reliable and trustworthy, and he will understand the value of his contribution to the company. He will be the marketing manager who works hard to make the deadline for the ad campaign. He will be the product developer who does not try to escape the blame for the last unsuccessful product, but makes it the inspiration for the next successful product. He will not dodge responsibility; he will enthusiastically accept it, and this will move both him and the company forward.

With a developed sense of empathy young people will make decisions that will forge important long-term relationships and be crucial to their careers. For example, something as simple as apologizing for being late shows they understand that their actions have made someone wait. This shows they value other people's time. Asking well in advance for time off for a doctor's appointment shows an employer that young people understand that their absence affects the productivity of others. These seem very simple, but they will go a long way in developing a respectful professional relationship. Those who have a developed sense of empathy also understand that how people think of us is based on their last interaction with us. Thus, when leaving a position, giving appropriate notice and helping to find and train a replacement will ensure that when looking for a new position, young people are able to get a good reference.

Consistent participation in the arts is a key way to foster these much needed accountability skills. While accountability is probably one of the more challenging skills to develop, if young people start practicing it early, they will be miles ahead of their peers. Future employers will surely take note of these advanced skills and these young people will be the ones who will not only rise to the top and achieve their goals, but will make the world a better place.

CHAPTER EIGHT

THE LOST ART OF CONVERSATION

They Text, They Tweet, But Can They Communicate?

Have you noticed that kids today spend more time texting and tweeting than talking? I am concerned that the time they spend communicating electronically rather than through face-to-face interactions, may be limiting their ability to communicate well. Many young people do not have the communication skills to express themselves effectively.

Nido Qubein, an internationally renowned speaker and business guru, explains that effective communication has three basic components: connecting with an audience, conveying messages the audience understands, and checking the audience's responses to what you are saying. Each of these components is crucial, and each of them requires a two-way connection between the speaker and the audience. Developing that connection requires a set of skills that is not developed through the kind of disjointed communication electronic interaction provides.

> *The single biggest problem in communication is the illusion that it has taken place.*
> **~George Bernard Shaw~**

On *The X-Factor* we hear Simon Cowell telling contestants to express the emotion of the song, so they can connect with the audience in a way that gives the audience goose bumps or makes them want to buy the song. Although Simon's responses are sometimes harsh, he teaches a valuable lesson about the importance of communication: in order to connect with an audience, the performer must be able to express herself effectively.

In the 1960s, researcher Albert Mehrabian conducted studies that pointed out the importance of non-verbal components in our interactions with others. Mehrabian's studies suggested that as much as 93% of our communication is channelled through something other than the words we choose to speak. He concluded that, in some situations, 55% of communication comes from body language, 38% comes from the tone of voice we use, and only 7% comes from the actual words we choose.

These numbers show that non-verbal communication carries more weight than verbal communication. When there is a contradiction between a person's verbal and non-verbal expression, it is more important (and effective) to pay attention to the non-verbal cues. Experience in the arts develops these important non-verbal communication skills.

EFFECTIVE COMMUNICATION AND THE LIMITS OF TECHNOLOGY

In some ways, technology helps us to be stronger communicators. It encourages us to communicate more often, and it gives us tools that allow us to communicate more easily. With our computers and our smartphones, we are almost never out of touch, and the intensity of our communication with others is much greater than it was before we had access to all this technology.

However, just because we interact more often than we used to, it does not mean that the quality of our interaction is better. The same technology that makes it easy for us to interact at any time, in any place, makes us lazy in our interactions. This laziness takes two forms. Firstly, we opt for messages that are abbreviated, simple and stripped of any extraneous thoughts—the kind of messages that get to the point and go no further.

Secondly, we tend to choose text messages over face-to-face contact or even a conversation on the phone. It is so much easier to send a quick text without having to deal with pleasantries and all the extra interaction that goes along with face-to-face communication. We avoid the emotions involved in face-to-face interactions and the possible unexpected responses we will have to react to. We choose the disjointed nature of text messaging because it allows us to avoid giving an immediate response. It gives us time to think and choose how we are going to answer, if at all.

In some cases, the 140-character limit on *Twitter* messages can be a constraint that actually stimulates creativity by forcing us to communicate our idea in a clear and concise way. The issue, however, is that there are many concepts and ideas that take many more than 140 characters to communicate. If youth are practicing communication mostly in text messages and tweets, they will struggle to hone the skills necessary to develop in-depth explanations of ideas.

Let us think about Qubein's important aspects of communication: connecting with our audience, delivering a message, and checking responses to what we are saying. Doing all of these things requires focus. They require us to be present, to listen, and to be attentive. None of this is possible with a text message, and relying heavily on electronic communication, results in poor development of these crucial skills.

When I am conducting interviews for staff, I see countless examples of young people who are unable to deliver a message and to express what they think or feel. I see so many youth who are not comfortable with face-to-face interaction, or simply do not understand how they come across. I have even had a university student come in for an interview wearing headphones and without even saying hello, proceed to plug in his cell phone to charge beside the interview table. It was shocking that he had no idea how unprofessionally he presented himself.

Many youth, especially in job interviews, are unaware of their fidgeting and lack of eye contact. They are often nervous and not able to present themselves as cool and collected. They are unaware of the importance of body language and tone of voice. They also struggle with responding on their feet. Their lack of practice with face-to-face communication, not only reduces their performance skills, it also reduces their ability to read others and pick up nuances of vocal tone and body language.

BONUS

For a list of my Top 10 Do's and Don'ts of a job interview scan here or visit:
www.theartisticedge.ca/thebook

THE ARTS AND COMMUNICATION

This is where the arts can help. The Washington State Arts Commission states that, "the arts are languages that all people speak—that cut across racial, cultural, social, educational, and economic barriers. They are symbol systems as important as letters and numbers. They integrate mind, body, and spirit and provide opportunities for self-expression, making it possible for abstractions to become more understandable as they take concrete form in the visual arts, music, dance and drama."

Once we understand that we can express emotion and tell stories without literally spelling them out in words, we can understand how art can be intensively expressive without using any words at all. Music students learn to comprehend the versatility of musical language; they come to understand how Beethoven can express grandeur and power in his Ninth Symphony, while

Tchaikovsky can use the same palette of notes to express plaintive sadness in *Swan Lake.*

In visual arts, non-verbal language is just as important. A painting like Edvard Munch's *The Scream* uses colour and gestural line and its subject's pose and facial expression to evoke the ideas of anguish and anxiety - all without employing a single word. When painting students understand how such a painting conveys meaning, they begin to understand how communication is about more than words.

The performing arts teach techniques to help students harness the power of non-verbal expression. Students begin to understand that there is a wealth of expression in movement, gesture, and facial expression. Learning how to recognize and interpret these non-verbal cues allows them to move beyond words to deeper and more complex levels of expression.

Theatre instructors are constantly asking their students to be aware of body language. Not only that, instructors ask their students to practice one role using many different kinds of body language with the goal of finding the most convincing delivery of the message they are trying to communicate to the audience. Thus, children start to view communication in more complex ways when they explore it through the arts.

Approaches such as *Laban Movement Analysis* emphasize careful observation of the subtleties of movement—how bodies move in relation to themselves, to other bodies, to the space around them—and what the nuances of movement can tell us about what those bodies are trying to express. These approaches are about status and how people move to convey their status. Learning these techniques helps students both to read the body language of others and to use their own body language to express themselves.

The Overcoat, a play loosely based on Nikolai Gogol's short stories, is an excellent example of how a theatre piece can communicate complex ideas and emotions without the use of words. I saw the production at *The Canadian Stage Company* in Toronto many years ago and I was absolutely stunned at the brilliance of it. A physical theatre piece, *The Overcoat* masterfully melds movement with music to tell a compelling story.

It is not just non-verbal communication that can be improved through the performing arts. Theatre training can also help students add nuances to spoken dialogue to give the text a deeper meaning than is obvious on the surface. Through adjusting phrasing, pacing, and variations in volume, a theatre student learns that often the most important aspect of his performance is not *what* he says, but *how* he says it. He learns that subtle changes in delivery—emphasis on certain words, speaking slowly or quickly, loudly or softly—can change the message he is conveying.

> *The most important thing in communication is hearing what isn't said.*
> **~Peter F. Drucker~**

It is incredible how intricate communication really is. Children would benefit greatly from spending more time developing their understanding of the art of communication. Imagine how much easier it would be to impress an employer with confident body language and to deliver a convincing answer as to why they are fit for the job.

THE COMMUNICATION GAP

"For more than 10 years, we've asked employers about key skills, and they have consistently named communication skills as critical, yet have also said this is something many candidates lack," said Marilyn Mackes, executive director of the National Association of Colleges and Employers in reference to a 2006 survey conducted by her organization.

In a 2007 article in the *Extension Journal* of the Rutgers University Cooperative Extension of Middlesex County, Laura Bovitz reported that 84% of teens owned a personal media device such as a computer or cell phone, 87% of teens used the internet, and of the teens who had an online presence, 75% preferred to use text messages to communicate rather than regular email.

A survey conducted in 2012 by marketing firm *AWeber Communications,* indicated that 93% of teens preferred to use their phones for communication, as opposed to 47% who used a video chat service such as Skype—a suggestion that kids are more comfortable sending texts than they are seeing—and being seen by—the person they are communicating with.

These statistics show how deeply young people rely on technology for their connection to the world. They would feel disconcertingly disconnected from everything and everyone if they lost their technology, and because they have grown up with access to it, they feel entitled to access it at all times. Make them face the possibility of losing one technological channel—texts or *Facebook* or *Twitter*—and they will find a new one rather than resort to a non-technological method of communication.

In order to be competitive in today's job market, young people need to be able to communicate well, and their reliance on communication technology is not helping them learn how to be good communicators. In addition to preventing them from learning to navigate the subtleties of non-verbal communication, their tech-centred world keeps them isolated, and they lose touch with the fact that there is a whole world out there that communicates in a very different way.

Teens who think that text messages allow them to communicate effectively, do not understand the complexity of communication. Texting eliminates non-verbal cues, which are significant indicator of what a person is trying to say. The language we use in texting is short and removed from a context, so it often carries a tone that we may not intend. This is the reason we need to add smiley faces to a message, to ensure our tone is not misinterpreted. The smiley face replaces the actual smile on our face.

Even in email communication, I find that the majority of people are not aware of how their communication style comes across. This disconnect between what young people are trying to express and their ability to express it effectively is a huge handicap, especially in the job market.

Young people know that their parents and teachers do not communicate the way they do, and they have little patience for adults who place more emphasis on non-technological forms of communication. Marketers know that in order to grab the attention of young people, they have to communicate with them in ways they understand.

"With younger generations entering the workforce and obtaining disposable income, marketers must take note of their communication patterns," explains Justin Premick, AWeber's Director of Education Marketing. "To sell to them, it's vitally important to speak their language."

What young people often fail to understand is that many of their potential bosses are also from a different generation whose communication styles are different from theirs. This means that not everyone is going to be willing to speak their tech-heavy language in order to communicate with them.

It takes two to tango, as the saying goes, so while there is a lot of information out there about how older generations can communicate and connect with Generation Z, it is also important that the current generation understands that not everyone speaks like them. They are going to have to communicate with their bosses to explain things, to ask for favours and to be effective in their job. If they cannot communicate in the ways that they need to communicate, their bosses will find someone who can.

> *To effectively communicate, we must realize that we are all different in the way we perceive the world and use this understanding as a guide to our communication with others.*
>
> **~Tony Robbins~**

There are many instances with my own camp staff when they ask for time off or a favour of some kind and their approach is more *telling me* than *asking me*. It is extremely frustrating, but after I take a deep breath, I actually coach them on how to ask their question in a way that is going to make me want to say yes. The arts are a fantastic training ground for young people to learn how the subtleties of communication affect their interactions with others and more importantly how others perceive them. Understanding how to use words and body language to our advantage is key to success in life. The arts teach this in countless ways.

CHAPTER NINE

CHANGE IS THE ONLY CONSTANT

Why Being Adaptable Matters Most

As I hope I have made clear so far in this book, the one thing we can count on as we move into the future is that the world is going to keep transforming around us. Technology, the marketplace and the demands placed on us by our careers will all remain in a constant state of change. In order for any of us to keep up, to remain competitive, and to be successful and happy, we will need the ability to adapt.

Of all the essential skills I have outlined in this book, adaptability is arguably the most important skill for young people to develop. Adaptability ensures children will be able to meet whatever challenges come their way, especially if those challenges arise unexpectedly, which they often do. However, if they pay attention to trends they will know how to adapt. If they adapt, they will be selected.

I have saved this most important skill for last because it is built on the other skills I have discussed up to this point. For example, the skill of creative thinking I outlined in chapter three, is a key component in being able to adapt to a new situation. Steve Jobs and *Apple* were able to adapt to a changing technological marketplace by thinking creatively as they developed new products. Similarly, the problem-solving skills I discussed in chapter five—being able to approach problems as opportunities rather than obstacles—allow young people to find new approaches instead of feeling stuck at the first sign of a challenge. This is all a part of adaptability—being able work with a situation that turns out differently than we initially anticipated.

It is a simple formula: add together problem-solving skills, creativity, confidence and a positive mindset. Voilà! You now have adaptability.

Adaptability does not come easily, however. It is so much easier to stick with what we know and leave things the way they are. Unfortunately, that is not an option anymore, when we consider the rapid pace at which the world is changing. Standing still is not going to lead us where we want to be. The job market is changing so fast and in so many ways; young people who are going to be looking for jobs in the near future need to be able to adapt constantly in order to keep up. If they try to maintain the status quo, they will surely be left behind. The environment of any given time determines what will be required for success, and adapting to what the environment calls for will help us to succeed.

> " It is not the strongest of the species that survives, nor the most intelligent that survives. It is the one that is the most adaptable to change.
> ~Charles Darwin~

KEEPING EDUCATION UP TO DATE

Daniel Pink claims that our current educational models are behind where they need to be to prepare our young people for the changes they are going to face in the marketplace of the future.

"It used to be that the abilities that mattered most at work, in business, in achieving professional success and personal fulfillment, were abilities that were characteristic of the left hemisphere of the brain—the logical, linear, sequential, analytical, spreadsheet, SAT, 'I know the right answer' abilities," he says. "Those abilities are still absolutely one hundred percent necessary today, but no longer sufficient. Abilities characteristic of the right hemisphere of the brain—artistry, empathy, inventiveness, big-picture thinking—these abilities are now the first among equals."

Some educational institutions cling to the old ways of doing things, and as a result are not preparing their students for the workplace of tomorrow or even the workplace of today. In a 2009 article in *Teacher Education Quarterly*, Shelley Sherman proposes that the way future teachers learnt during their own schooling affects how they teach during their career. This is a logical argument as to why schools cannot keep up. Generally, those who choose to be teachers go through a short training period and then are certified to begin teaching. As children, however, we have spent our formative years in school learning in a certain way. Sherman says, "Although many teacher education programs may promote progressive practice, it can be quite challenging for such programs to have an impact on the beliefs of teacher candidates who are so accustomed themselves to being taught in certain ways."

Many industries and job markets change so quickly now that there is no way to know how the situation in a given field is going to change by the time a student finishes a four-year degree. Depending on the field the student is entering, they are likely to emerge from university to find a job market nothing at all like the market they thought they were preparing themselves for when they began their studies.

Even after a person has worked in an industry for several years, it is not uncommon for things to change, leaving them stranded. They can suddenly find that their industry has shifted and what they studied—the skills they learned years ago—are no longer relevant. Even worse, the industry may shift directions, so that their actual job position may suddenly cease to exist. Think back to the days when everybody used film. The invention of digital photography wiped out an entire industry. Kodak was forced to adapt to the changes in the market and ultimately closed its film factories.

One thing is certain: career stability is a thing of the past. Canada's Labour Ministry reports that today's typical Canadian worker will have an average of eight jobs in three different careers over the course of his lifetime. In America, the situation is even more dramatic; a 2010 Bureau of Labor Statistics study found that workers between the ages of eighteen and forty-four had held an average eleven different jobs, and a quarter of those workers had had fifteen or more jobs. With the proliferation of continuing education programs at universities, the message is clear: "Keep up, or retrain and start again."

Since I started my own company in 2008, there have been significant changes in the vision and approach to achieving my goals. It has been a major lesson in adaptability for me. I have learned to embrace this change with open arms because the alternative would have kept me stuck in a business model that no longer works. Times have changed and the market tells us when something does not work—we just have to listen. Let's be honest: it is not always easy to see

> *If you do not change direction, you may end up where you are heading.*
> ~Lao Tzu~

what is staring us in the face. Sometimes it takes someone else to point out to us what does not work. I have to thank Raymond Aaron for so clearly pointing out the flaws in my own business structure. Had I been reluctant to heed his advice, I would have headed down a path to bankruptcy.

HOW THE ARTS CAN HELP

As Daniel Pink points out, the most important skills that will allow young people to adapt to the changing job marketplace are creative, right brain skills. The preceding chapters have aimed at explaining how arts education helps to hone those right brain skills. The arts play a key role in bringing all those skills together to help children be flexible and adaptable, which is precisely what they need to be in order to succeed.

Experiences in the arts help us build adaptability in several different ways:

Through Improvisation

Many art forms, especially in the performing arts, expect participants to be able to move forward without a set plan to guide them, to apply their skills to a changing situation on the fly. When we are involved in improvisation in any art discipline, we do not know what is going to happen, so it is essential that we are able deal with whatever may happen.

One of my favourite forms of dance is salsa. I have been training in salsa along with many other Latin dances for over two years now. When dancers build skills and techniques in salsa dancing, they have a set of moves or sequences they know. When they come together with a dance partner and start dancing there is no choreography. They do not talk. They do not plan. They just react to the music and to the lead their partner gives them. They use the set of moves they know to react to what their partner does.

When I first started salsa dancing I found this extremely challenging. No choreography? Most of the styles of dance I had done in the past were all choreographed. Learning to follow the signals my dance partner was giving me took months and months to develop. As if that were not challenging enough, every partner leads differently. I remember the first time I went to a salsa club, I was so thrown off because each man I danced with led very differently from my instructor. I had to adapt to each of their styles or I would not know what to do. My passion for salsa dancing became a lesson in adaptability because it consistently forced me to improvise.

Experience in improvisation is important for two reasons:

1. We have the opportunity to practice paying attention to others in our environment, observing and reacting and maybe even predicting trends. This skill is vital in adapting to changes in life and work, particularly as young people begin their careers. Experience in the arts gives us multiple opportunities to practice this skill in many different environments with many different people. The arts help us to hone our skill of observation, which is a mental habit that will serve us in other contexts. With practice, we do not get tripped up or stalled by unexpected changes. We just react using one of the sets of moves we have developed. Also, with more experience we see there are no unexpected changes. Change is normal and expected.

2. With more experience we continually learn new sets of moves we can use to react to different situations. With training in improvisation, we learn how to develop a storehouse of skills that we can put away until we need them. When an unexpected situation arises, we have a wealth of experience we can draw upon to help us to address the new challenge that is suddenly in front of us.

Through Exploring Creativity

There are as many versions of expressing a single idea as there are artists. As I described in chapter three, in art there is no 'perfect', and in many cases, there is no 'right answer'. Academic learning typically conditions us to think that there is a correct answer to every question. If we are only trained in academics, we do not know what to do when the formulae we have been taught do not produce the right answer to a new problem. An arts education, on the other hand, teaches us that there can be multiple 'right' answers to a question, and there is not always a formula that will give us the solution.

In a 2002 article entitled, *The State of the Arts and The Improvement of Education,* Elliot Eisner, one of the most quoted experts in arts education, explains that creating art is valuable because it gives young people experience in an environment where imagination is celebrated, multiple solutions are encouraged, and where the fact that the answer is unknown is appreciated.

Knowing this not only encourages us to be creative and strive to do better, it also encourages us to try to present something in a different way than others. Calculus is calculus; there is no way around it. Calculus is a technique for solving one type of problem. It is a tool and nothing more. Each person who uses it will get the same answer. On the other hand, a painting of a sunset will never be the same twice. There are tools such as colour mixing and brush strokes that help create the image, but each person will create their own version of the same sunset. Understanding this encourages children to find solutions to problems that are new and different, instead of trying to find the same solution that everyone before them has found.

I am not saying that science and math are not creative fields. Physicists and scientists use creativity to solve problems every day. It is the way these subjects are sometimes taught to our children that is the problem. In math class, typically students take in information and practice using formulae. Math education for children is all about learning a technique for problem-solving and then applying that technique in a certain, predefined way. Rarely do they have a chance to experiment with these formulae. Learning technique is also important in art, but with a good teacher, equal time should be spent on learning the creative ways we can use that technique to achieve new results.

Through Practicing Flexibility

The process of art making is unpredictable. Part of this process is making mistakes and adapting to them. An actor did not get the part he wanted in a play. A dancer is dancing with a new partner. An artist's original idea for a sculpture has to be changed because of the limitations of the materials she wanted to use. In visual art, situations like this force us to either, adapt our vision, work within the limitations of what the material can do, or choose a new material that will suit our vision. In theatre, we will learn to inhabit a new character. In dance, as I did, we learn to adjust our dance style to fit the energy of our new partner.

Take for example, the role of a "swing". Most of the big Broadway productions have swings. Their job is to know several roles within the show so if someone gets sick they can fill in. Swings are the best adapters. They go from a standing start, not having rehearsed for that specific role in several weeks, and with a quick refresher the day of the show they are able to do what they need to do in order to adjust and fill in. Those who are fit for this role will perform as if they were always meant to play that part. The trick is adapting smoothly. If they do it well, it appears as if they have always been cast in that role. They get used to thinking on their feet. That is life—we have to know how to swing!

THE CONFIDENCE TO ADAPT

In any kind of performance, it helps to practice imagining things through beforehand. What will happen during the performance? What could go wrong? What could change during the performance? Imagining these potential changes helps a performer to anticipate those changes as a normal reality, and that in turn helps her not to be surprised when they come. Performances are unpredictable, and young people should learn to embrace the unexpected twists rather than fear them.

> " You must be the change you wish to see in the world.
> ~Mahatma Gandhi~

It is critical that young people become used to the idea of change so that it does not paralyze them when it happens—because it *will* happen. Each time they adjust and adapt to something unexpected, they gain experience in thinking on their feet. They learn how to trust their skills. Adaptability is strongly tied to confidence in one's ability. With practice, they will be confident they have the tools to successfully roll with whatever happens.

In dance and improv theatre, we are told to stop thinking and just react. Don't sweat the small stuff; just accept the changes and move on. When we combine that kind of flexibility with a strong sense of confidence, we are able to handle whatever comes our way, no matter how unexpected it might be. It is a skill that is essential in the arts—one that is easily built through participation in the arts—and it is a skill that will serve young people well as they move out into the swift current of our rapidly changing world.

CHAPTER TEN

THE CURTAIN CALL

All the skills I have described in this book fall into the category of Leadership Skills. I wanted to focus on these because they are not always given the emphasis they deserve in our current education systems. The arts are an excellent way to develop this skill set, but it is more complex than simply enrolling a child in just any arts program.

There are two closing concepts that I want to leave you with as you consider the ideas I have discussed throughout these pages. The first is that only consistent practice will develop all the skills that are key to success in life. The second is that leadership skills really only stick when facilitators are intentional about teaching them.

PRACTICE

We have all heard the phrase "Practice makes perfect". However, many arts educators do not like to use the term 'perfect'. They do not believe in it. What does 'perfect' look like? Most of art is so subjective that it is not realistic to define perfection. Therefore, when there is no perfect, there is always a way to do better. Thus, if we focus on the concept of 'practice', it will drive us closer to the goals we want to achieve.

In Malcolm Gladwell's book *Outliers: The Story of Success*, he repeatedly mentions the "10,000-Hour Rule", stating that the key to success in any field is, to a large extent, a matter of practicing a specific task for a total of about 10,000 hours. I love this concept!

No one questions the need to practice when learning an instrument. I believe the same practice must be applied in developing leadership skills. Life is complex and always changing. Developing the skills to manage this complexity takes years of practice. We cannot expect young people to become good leaders as soon as they enter the job market anymore than we could expect them to be proficient piano players the day after they start playing.

As I've mentioned before, I have conducted hundreds of job interviews over the years and one thing that consistently sticks out is how unprepared young people are to sell themselves. It is frustrating to watch them fumble over their words when I know that all they need is some coaching and a lot of practice. Why don't we have teenagers participating in weekly lessons where they can practice interview and presentation skills just as they would piano? The point is, these abilities do not happen overnight.

At my summer camp we have integrated this type of training through our counsellor-in-training program. The teens in this program have mock job interviews with me and then get instant feedback and coaching on how they did and which areas they could improve. One of areas I work on with them is how to explain the value of their experiences. This is something most young people struggle to do well.

The problem is, while young people *are* developing valuable skills at school and in their extra-curricular activities, they spend little time developing leadership skills. The focus is on academics, and leadership is largely an afterthought. There is a general misconception that leadership skills should be absorbed naturally as part of growing up. The reality is, they need to be taught and practiced like any other skill.

I hear about schools taking their students on a three-to-five day leadership retreat at the beginning of the school year. This is a fantastic start, and such a great way for young people to forge connections with their fellow students and teachers. However, I wonder if those schools continue the development of leadership skills when they get back to the city and into the classroom? My guess is that in many cases, the priorities switch back to math, science and English, or whatever core subjects students are being tested on. To be fair, the pressure on teachers to increase their school's test scores is always high and teachers are so busy that there is little time to focus on leadership skill development.

Parents, on the other hand, generally trust that their children are learning these skills at school and are sometimes surprised when they leave school and are not able to cope well. Young people are finishing school, whether high school or university, with a whole set of skills that are sadly underdeveloped, and these are skills crucial to their success. Tony Wagner, author of *The Global Achievement Gap,* says, "Students are simply not learning the skills that matter most for the twenty-first century."

In chapter three, I spoke about the changing global job market and the necessity for our young people to stand out in a crowd of potential employees that now includes citizens of nearly every country on the planet. The only way they will stand out is if they have skills that global workers do not have. Well-developed leadership skills are a platform that makes a job candidate stand taller than everyone around him.

Participation in the arts is such a fantastic way for young people to consistently practice leadership skills. I have explained throughout the book how participation in the arts demands a set of skills that is crucial to effective leadership—reliability, respect for the work of others, empathy, confidence, adaptability and so much more—and these are precisely the skills young people will need the most as they enter a fiercely competitive job market. As they perform and rehearse, young people will be practicing skills they will be asked to use on the job, and when the time comes to put those leadership skills to work, they will be ready.

Perhaps the biggest result of participation in the arts is the development of creative thinking and problem-solving skills. With every artistic project a child undertakes—whether it is a role in a play, a dance routine or a painting—she will be asked to come up with her own creative solution to the problems that are put in front of her. She will have to decide where she wants to go with her creation, will be encouraged to think creatively as she comes up with her answers and will be rewarded when she is innovative. She will go through this process over and over again, practicing for the challenges that lie ahead in her life. By practicing these skills early through the arts, she is giving herself the competitive edge she needs to compete.

IT'S ALL ABOUT INTENTION

In addition to practice, an equally important element to learning these skills through arts education, is intention. Are the dance, music, theatre and art teachers intentional about teaching the leadership skills that can be developed through the arts? I would argue that if the instructors are not intentional, leadership skill development will not be as strong as it could be.

Michael Brandwein, whom I have mentioned a few times throughout my book, first introduced me to the idea of intentionality. He speaks about the idea of an "intentional camp". He explains that what most camps emphasize on their websites is *fun, friends and memories* to last a lifetime. However, the true business of camp is (or should be) youth development and teaching kids skills for life. Michael says, "Fun is not the mission. Fun is what it feels like as we accomplish the mission." This implies the purpose of an activity should never just be to have fun, but there should be a learning objective that the participants have 'fun' accomplishing.

The U.S. *National Association for the Education of Young Children*, in its guide for intentional teaching, explains how intentional teaching is, by definition, the product of careful planning and preparation.

"To be 'intentional' is to act purposefully," the guide explains, "with a goal in mind and a plan for accomplishing it. Intentional acts originate from careful thought and are accompanied by consideration of their potential effects."

When done correctly, intentional teaching is a very efficient process of connection between the teacher and the student. The teacher is ready to seize every opportunity to teach the desired skills, and with every 'teachable moment', the student gains more practice at exercising that skill.

"Intentional teaching does not happen by chance; it is planful, thoughtful, and purposeful," says the NAEYC. "Intentional teachers use their knowledge, judgment, and expertise to organize learning experiences for children; when an unexpected situation arises (as it always does), they can recognize a teaching opportunity and are able to take advantage of it, too."

The facilitators of arts programs must understand the importance of being intentional about teaching all of the skills I have talked about, because it is crucial that our children have these skills in order to be successful later in life. Unless we as facilitators and teachers mindfully and deliberately work to build these skills when we have the chance, our young people are going to end up with poorly developed leadership skills, and will struggle to compete in the global marketplace. If, on the other hand, we make sure our kids are practicing these skills every step of the way, for hours and hours as they work in our programs, we can be sure we are giving them the edge they will need to succeed.

This idea truly resonates with me. In my own company, we have started to become extremely intentional about the skills children learn through our programs. We use every opportunity to have 'teachable moments' with the young people we work with. In staff training we talk about turning basic conversations into opportunities to teach young people about life. Whether it is in our private coaching program or our summer camp, we intentionally teach leadership skills through our artistic programming by asking questions.

Asking questions allows teachers to point children toward a goal, but it leaves the responsibility for thinking and discovering answers in the hands of the student. Asking questions is an especially powerful tool in the arts because the creative thinking the question inspires is such an important skill for the student to have. In visual art, it may be that teachers ask, "Why did you choose that colour?" or "How is the person that you drew feeling?" In an improv exercise, they might ask, "How did you decide who would start the scene?" As the student works to discover the answers to these questions, he is practicing his creative-thinking skills.

It should not be assumed that just because someone teaches the arts he or she fully understands the depth of what children can learn from the experience. Teachers must be taught how to facilitate in such a way that they give their students the opportunity to practice these crucial skills. They must know how to recognize and react to teachable moments. They must know what skills they are trying to teach, and they must know the appropriate challenges to put in front of their students so that they are encouraged to practice the skills.

SO HOW DO WE KNOW?

So how do we know that young people are developing these skills? What are the indicators that adults will see to let them know that a child is developing their creativity, confidence or relationship building skills? Brandwein says we know by what children do or say.

In staff training at my summer camp, we review lists of what young people might do or say so we can clearly identify the skill being developed. This recognition is so important because it is an opportunity for positive reinforcement. If we praise the behaviour, we can further enhance its development. It is always so easy to identify skills that we do not want to see in young people, and we always seem to be specific about them. It is harder to be specific about skills we *do* want to see.

To illustrate, I thought I would share with you some of the lists that my staff and I have developed to help us identify leadership skills and encourage their development.

DEVELOPING CREATIVITY

HOW WILL YOU KNOW?
- They initiate new ideas.
- They express ideas in unique ways and from diverse perspectives.
- They seek to make their piece or performance different from others.
- They use something in a new way or for a different purpose.
- They are intensely curious.
- They are always thinking about options and possibilities as they approach a problem.
- They take positive risks when trying to solve a problem.
- They like to think independently and come up with their own solutions.
- They are not deterred by failure, and they keep working toward a solution.
- They like to improvise and experiment.

DEVELOPING CONFIDENCE

HOW WILL YOU KNOW?
- They volunteer opinions and ideas.
- They walk with their head high and a smile on their face.
- They are willing to try new things.
- They are comfortable meeting new people.
- They ask questions and are not afraid to admit when they do not know something.
- They answer questions without hesitation.
- They initiate conversations and introduce new topics.
- They accept criticism gracefully.

- They are relaxed in unfamiliar situations.
- They are not afraid to say "no".

DEVELOPING PROBLEM-SOLVING SKILLS

HOW WILL YOU KNOW?
- They approach a problem as an exciting challenge.
- They focus on the solution rather than on the problem.
- They analyze a problem by asking relevant questions.
- They are able to make complex choices by weighing possible solutions in light of the context.
- They are open to trying multiple ideas until a solution is found.
- They do not waste time trying to place blame for the problem.
- They remain neutral as they think of the problem; they do not see it as a personal attack.
- They are able to focus on the root of the problem so that they can find the simplest solution.
- They keep an open mind and do not discard possible solutions without serious consideration.
- They think creatively as they search for a solution.

DEVELOPING A POSITIVE MINDSET IN ORDER TO DREAM BIG

HOW WILL YOU KNOW?
- They see challenges as opportunities.
- They do not focus on the negativity around them from peers, family or society.
- They choose to surround themselves with positive people who turn dreams into reality.

- They welcome constructive criticism.
- They offer constructive support to others.
- They are focused and dedicated as they work on a project.
- They are aware of their strengths, and they look for ways to capitalize on them.
- They set goals and persistently work toward them.
- They do not dwell on problems, but instead focus on finding solutions.
- They are eager to try again when they fail.
- They strive to find the best qualities in people and situations.

DEVELOPING COMMUNICATION SKILLS

HOW WILL YOU KNOW?
- They walk tall without hunching over.
- They stand with their arms uncrossed.
- They make eye contact during interactions with people they meet.
- They use their facial expressions to express positivity.
- They speak clearly and confidently.
- They respond enthusiastically and appropriately to questions.
- They initiate interactions.
- They ask questions and listen to the answers.
- They show interest in others and do not monopolize conversations.

DEVELOPING RELATIONSHIP BUILDING SKILLS

HOW WILL YOU KNOW?

- They think about how their actions affect others around them.
- They offer help when they see someone needs it.
- They do something nice for a friend or co-worker without being asked.
- They are willing to discuss conflicts openly and honestly.
- They emphasize the positive aspects of their relationships rather than the negative.
- They fulfill their responsibilities when working in a group.
- They are respectful and supportive of everyone around them.
- They are consistent and reliable in their interactions with others.
- They are honest and open.
- They treat others with respect.
- They give others the chance to take on a leadership role.

DEVELOPING ACCOUNTABILITY

HOW WILL YOU KNOW?

- They are committed to being on time and prepared.
- They do not want to miss a rehearsal because they are aware that this will make things difficult for others in the group.
- They are willing to admit they made a mistake.
- They are willing to use mistakes as an opportunity to improve.
- They are willing to apologize sincerely when they have done something wrong.

- They do not shift the blame to others when they are responsible for something going wrong.
- They are eager to take on responsibility in the group.
- They work to make the whole group successful, not just themselves.
- They are honest as they try to figure out why something went wrong.
- They accept criticism without anger or excuses.

DEVELOPING ADAPTABILITY

HOW WILL YOU KNOW?

- They show they understand that change is a part of life by being open when unexpected situations arise.
- They do not resist changes in rules or procedures.
- They work to make changes work instead of focusing on why the change will not work.
- They can adjust their priorities when situations change.
- They see new situations as opportunities and they are excited when they get the chance to learn from a new situation.
- They help others to deal with change.
- They quickly learn to use new tools in innovative ways.
- They can adjust their way of working when the situation demands it.

So how do we use these lists?

I encourage you to pay closer attention as you interact with the children in your life. Notice things that they do or say that show you they are developing these important skills. I am willing to bet, that if we start to notice these qualities in young people and praise them, we will see them developing stronger leadership skills.

BONUS

 The way that we praise young people is important. If you would like to learn more about how to deliver specific praise that will develop leadership skills, scan here, or visit www.theartisticedge.ca/thebook

As the curtain falls on this final page of my book, I hope you have discovered new strategies by which you can develop leadership in the children you interact with each day. Whether we are parents, educators or arts instructors, there is so much we can do to prepare our children to achieve success in life. We can make intentional choices and choose activities that will help the young people we interact with, stand out, be heard and dream big—for that is what they need to succeed in today's society. Choose the arts, and give them *the artistic edge.*

NOTES

References appear in order of mention. Please note that every effort was made to find the sources for quoted material. Should you have any information that will increase the accuracy of the sources listed please contact the author.

Chapter 1

Innovation Skills Profile: The Skills, Attitudes, and Behaviours You Need to Contribute to Innovation in the Workplace. Rep. Toronto, ON: Conference Board of Canada, 2011 Retrieved from: <http://www.conferenceboard.ca/education>.

Campbell, S., & Townshend, K., *Making a case for arts education.* Toronto, ON: Ontario Arts Council, 1997.

Insights and Observations About Generation Z. Grail Research Analysis, 2011. Retrieved from <http://www.grailresearch.com>.

Oblinger, Diana, and James L. Oblinger. *Educating the Net Generation.* Boulder, CO: EDUCAUSE, 2005.

Mamen, Maggie. *The Pampered Child Syndrome: How to Recognize It, How to Manage It, and How to Avoid It : A Guide for Parents and Professionals.* London: J. Kingsley, 2006.

Chapter 2

Upitis, Rena. *Arts Education for the Development of the Whole Child.* Prepared for the Elementary Teachers' Federation of Ontario, Canada. 2011.

Ornstein, Robert E. *The Right Mind: Making Sense of the Hemispheres.* New York: Harcourt Brace, 2001.

Jensen, Eric P. "A Fresh Look at Brain-Based Education." *Phi Delta Kappa International* 6. 89 (2008): 408-17. *Education Resources Information Center.* Web. 05 Aug. 2012.

Graham, Judith, and Leslie Forstadt, Ph.D. "Children and Brain Development: What We Know About How Children Learn." *The University of Maine—Cooperative Extension Publications.* The University of Maine, 2011. Web. 15 Oct. 2012. <http://umaine.edu/publications/4356e/>.

Pink, Daniel H. *A Whole New Mind: Why Right-brainers Will Rule the Future.* New York: Riverhead, 2006.

Greenough, William. "We Can't Focus Just on Ages Zero to Three." *APA Monitor* 28.19 (1997).

Richards, Thomas A., Phd. "Social Anxiety, Chemical Imbalances, Neural Pathways and Associations in the Brain." *The Social Anxiety Institute*, 2012. Web. 16 Sept. 2012. <http://www.socialanxietyinstitute.org/chemical.html>.

Baum, Susan, Steven Owen, and Barry Oreck. "Transferring Individual Self-regulation Processes from Arts to Academics." *Arts Education Policy Review* 98.4 (1997): 32-39.

Hetland, Lois. *Studio Thinking: The Real Benefits of Visual Arts Education.* New York: Teachers College, 2007.

"Artful Thinking." *Artful Thinking.* Harvard Graduate School of Education, 2010. Web. 16 May 2012. <http://www.pz.harvard.edu/Research/ArtThink.htm>.

Ritchhart, Ron, Patricia Palmer, Mark Church, and Shari Tishman. *Thinking Routines: Establishing Patterns of Thinking in the Classroom*. Rep. Prepared for the AERA Conference: Harvard Graduate School of Education, 2006. Web. 16 May 2012 <http://www.pz.harvard.edu/Research/ArtThink.htm>.

JWT Mumbai, India. "Beans & Beyond: Extra Strong Coffee." Ads of the World™, Dec. 2009. Web. 28 Sept. 2012. <http://adsoftheworld.com/media/print/beans_beyond_extra_strong_coffee>.

Chapter 3

Pink, Daniel H. *A Whole New Mind: Why Right-brainers Will Rule the Future*. New York: Riverhead, 2006.

Moncarz, Roger J., Michael G. Wolf, and Benjamin Wright. "Service-providing Occupations, Offshoring, and the Labor Market." *Monthly Labor Review* 12th ser. 131, December (2008): 71-86.

Valentino-DeVries, Jennifer. "Steve Jobs's Best Quotes." Web log post. *Digits, WSJ Blogs*. The Wall Street Journal, 24 Aug. 2011. Web. 26 July 2012. <http://blogs.wsj.com/digits/2011/08/24steve-jobss-best-quotes/>.

Sinek, Simon. *Start with Why: How Great Leaders Inspire Everyone to Take Action*. New York: Portfolio, 2009.

Elliot, Amy-Mae. "15 Digital Agency Work Spaces That Evoke Creativity." *Mashable*, 29 Aug. 2011. Web. 3 Aug. 2012. <http://mashable.com/2011/08/29/digital-agency-offices/>.

Robinson, Ken. *Out of Our Minds: Learning to Be Creative*. Oxford: Capstone, 2001.

Chapin, Harry. "Flowers Are Red." *HarryChapin.com*. The Harry Chapin Archive, 2009. Web. 1 May 2012. <http://harrychapin.com/music/flowers.shtml>.

Phillips, Lisa. "Learning How To Learn From The Masters: Lisa Phillips Interviews Michael Brandwein." *The Artistic Edge*. Web. 8 May 2012. <http://theartisticedge.ca>.

Chapter 4

Pacino, Al. "View All Al Pacino Quotes." *Search Quotes*. n.d. Web. 22 Aug. 2012. <http://www.searchquotes.com/quotation/My_first_language_was_shy._Its_only_by_having_been_thrust_into_the_limelight_that_I_have_learned_to_/275868/>.

Brooks, Katharine. *You Majored in What?: Mapping Your Path from Chaos to Career*. New York, NY: Viking, 2009.

Smith, Jacquelyn. "How To Be More Confident At Work." *Forbes*. Forbes Magazine, 06 Mar. 2012. Web. 26 Sept. 2012. <http://www.forbes.com/sites/jacquelynsmith/2012/03/06/how-to-be-more-confident-at-work/>.

Brandwein, Michael. *Super Staff SuperVision: A How-to Handbook of Powerful Techniques to Lead Camp Staff to be their Best*. Lincolnshire, IL: Brandwein, 2002.

Stephens, Karen. "Twenty Ways to Encourage." *Parenting Exchange: Child Care Information Exchange,* Aug. 2004: 1-2. Web. 3 Sept. 2012<http://www.dpi.wi.gov/ccic/pdf/weekly_articles/twenty_ways_to_encourage.pdf>.

Chapter 5

Qubein, Nido. Unpublished Video Montage of Nido Qubein Key Note Speeches, viewed on November 27, 2011 at "Brand Your Way to Wealth Conference" The Raymond Aaron Group: Toronto, ON.

Assaraf, John. "Repeat Your Affirmations Daily." *John Assaraf*. John Assaraf, n.d. Web. 26 Sept. 2012.

<http://www.johnassaraf.com/law-of-attraction-2/repeat-your-affirmations-daily/>.

Hughes, Fergus P. "Spontaneous Play in the 21st Century." *Contemporary Perspectives on Play in Early Childhood Education.* Ed. Olivia N. Saracho and Bernard Spodek. Greenwich, CT: Information Age Pub., 2003: 21-39. Retrieved from: <http://www.uwgb.edu/hughesf/Spontaneous%20Play%20.htm>

Davis, Brent, and Dennis J. Sumara. *Complexity and Education: Inquiries into Learning, Teaching, and Research.* Mahwah, NJ: Lawrence Erlbaum Associates, 2006.

Randi Korn & Associates, Inc. *Educational Research: The Art of Problem Solving.* Rep. Vol. 1. New York, NY: Solomon R. Guggenheim Museum, 2010. Retrieved from: <http://www.guggenheim.org/new-york/education/school-educator-programs/learning-through-art/research-studies/art-of-problem-solving>.

Chapter 6

James, Catterall S., Dumais A. Susan, and Gillian Hampden-Thompson. *The Arts and Achievement in At-risk Youth: Findings from Four Longitudinal Studies.* Rep. no. 55. Washington, DC: National Endowment for the Arts, 2012. Retrieved from: <http://www.nea.gov/news/news12/Arts-At-Risk-Youth.html>.

Upitis, R., Smithrim, K., Patteson, A., & Meban, M. "The effects of an enriched elementary arts education program on teacher development, artist practices, and student achievement: Baseline student achievement and teacher data from six Canadian sites." *International Journal of Education and the Arts, 2.*8 (2001). Retrieved from <http://ijea.asu.edu/v2n8/>.

Patterson, Anne. "Research and Assessment: Learning Through the Arts." *Royal Conservatory of Music: Learning Through the*

Arts. Royal Conservatory of Music, n.d. Web. 14 Sept. 2012. <http://learning.rcmusic.ca/learning-through-arts/about-ltta/ assessment-and-evaluation>.

PBS Parents. "Tony DiTerlizzi and Encouraging Young Artists." *Posts in Encouraging Young Artists Category* PBS, 09 Oct. 2009. Web. 16 Sept. 2012. <http://www.pbs.org/parents/supersisters/ archives/encouraging-young-artists/>.

Maria, Passcuci. "Dream the Improbable." *The Buffalo News.* 28 Nov. 2004. Web. 7 Sept. 2012. <http://www.creativetypeco.com/ articles_dream.shtml>.

Free the Children. "Our Founders." Free The Children, Web. 3 Sept. 2012. <http://www.freethechildren.com/about-us/our-team/ our-founders/>.

Chapter 7

McGregor, Jena. "How Failure Breeds Success." *Bloomberg Business Weekly Magazine* 09 July 2006: *Bloomberg.* Web. 07 Sept. 2012. <http://www.businessweek.com/stories/2006-07-09/ how-failure-breeds-success>.

Hassel, Holly and Jessica Lourey. "The Dea(r)th of Student Responsibility." *College Teaching.* 53.1, (2005).

Manzana, Ehrine. "Harvard Prof. Decries Grade Inflation Trend." *The Chicago Maroon.* The University of Chicago, 18 May 2001. Web. 7 Sept. 2012. <http://chicagomaroon.com/2001/05/18/ harvard-prof-decries-grade-inflation-trend/>.

"Bus Monitor Bullying Video." *Wikipedia.* Wikimedia Foundation, 13 Oct. 2012. Web. 16 Oct. 2012. <http://en.wikipedia. org/wiki/Bus_monitor_bullying_video>.

Erika, Christakis. "Too Busy for a Summer Job? Why America's Youth Lacks Basic Work Skills." *Time Magazine: Ideas.*

Time, 1 May 2012. Web. 3 May 2012. http://ideas.time. com/2012/05/01/too-busy-for-a-summer-job-why-americas-youth-lacks-basic-worth-skills/#ixzz29Uf5Pj00>.

Landro, Laura. "Poetry, Painting to Earn an M.D." *The Wall Street Journal.* Dow Jones & Company, 1 Feb. 2011. Web. 17 Sept. 2012. <http://online.wsj.com/article/SB100014240527487046 80604576110240337491446.html?mod=rss_Health>.

"Art: Success Through Failure." *Time Magazine* 19 Mar. 1955. Web. 7 Sept. 2012. <http://www.time.com/time/magazine/article/0,9171,937184,00.html>.

Chapter 8

Qubein, Nido R. *How to Be a Great Communicator: In Person, on Paper, and on the Podium.* New York: J. Wiley, 1997.

Thompson, Jeff. "Is Nonverbal Communication a Numbers Game? Is Body Language Really over 90% of How We Communicate?" *Beyond Words: The Science and Fun of Non-Verbal Communication.* Psychology Today, 30 Sept. 2011. Web. 7 Sept. 2012. <http:// www.psychologytoday.com/blog/beyond-words/201109/ is-nonverbal-communication-numbers-game>.

Mehrabian, A., *Nonverbal Communication.* New Brunswick: Aldine Transaction. 1972.

Washington State Arts Commission, "Stimulating the Brain and Senses Through Art": 2003 Web. 03 Sept. 2011. <http://www. arts.wa.gov/resources/documents/WSAC-Winter-2003-Newsletter.pdf>.

"Employers Cite Communication Skills as Key, But Say Many Job Seekers Are Lacking." World at Work: Total Rewards Associations, 27 Apr. 2006. Web. 12 Sept. 2012. <http://www.worldatwork.org/waw/Content/jobcenter/html/article-38.html>.

Bovitz, Laura. "In Their Own Words--Understanding the Communication Styles of Teens." *Journal of Extension* 45.2 (2007): Web. <http://www.joe.org/joe/2007april/tt1.php>.

"How Do Teens Communicate? Infographic and Marketing Analysis." *AWeber Communications*, 2012. Web. 16 Sept. 2012. <http://www.aweber.com/blog/email-marketing/teens-communicate-infographic.htm>.

"How Do Teens Communicate? Email Remains The Leading Tool For America's Youth." *AWeber Communications*, 2012. Web. Sept. 2012. <http://www.aweber.com/blog/press/how-do-teens-communicate-email-remains-the-leading-tool-for-americas-youth>.

Chapter 9

Pink, Daniel. "Daniel Pink: Session Summary, 'Left-brain' vs. 'right-brain' Thinking." *White Papers: Daniel Pink's Presentation to The Masters Forum.* MVP Marketing + Design, Inc., n.d. Web. 11 Aug. 2012. <http://www.mvpdesign.com/press/white-papers.aspx>.

Sherman, S. "Haven't we seen this before? Sustaining a vision in teacher education for progressive teaching practice." *Teacher Education Quarterly,* 36.4 (2006): 41-60.

"The Changing Face of Canadian Workplaces." *Federal Labour Standards Review Commission.* Canadian Ministry of Labour, Dec. 2004. Web. 9 Sept. 2012. <http://www.hrsdc.gc.ca/eng/labour/employment_standards/fls/resources/resource01.shtml>.

Bureau of Labor Statistics. U.S. Department of Labor. *Number of Jobs Held, Labor Market Activity and Earnings Growth Among the Youngest Baby Boomers: Results from a Longitudinal Survey. National Longitudinal Surveys.* Bureau of Labor Statistics, 25

July 2012. Web. 9 Sept. 2012. <http://www.bls.gov/nls/nls-faqs.htm#anch41>.

Eisner, E. W. "The state of the Arts and the Improvement of Education." *Art Education Journal,* 1.1 (2002): 2-6.

Chapter 10

Gladwell, Malcolm. *Outliers: The Story of Success.* New York: Little, Brown and Company, 2008.

Wagner, Tony. *The Global Achievement Gap: Why Even Our Best Schools Don't Teach the New Survival Skills Our Children Need-- and What We Can Do about It.* New York: Basic, 2008.

Epstein, Ann S. *The Intentional Teacher: Choosing the Best Strategies for Young Children's Learning.* Washington, DC: National Association for the Education of Young Children, 2007. Retrieved from <http://www.naeyc.org/store/files/store/TOC/165.pdf>.

ABOUT THE AUTHOR

Lisa Phillips is the founder & CEO of Canada's Academy of Stage and Studio Arts and has been an arts educator and leadership professional for sixteen years. Her involvement in summer camps spans twenty-five years in both Canada and the United States, of which ten years has been as a camp director. Horizon Arts Camp was Lisa's first entrepreneurial adventure, which is now in its fifth season of giving young people incredible experiences in the arts and leadership development.

Lisa holds a degree in Psychology along with post-graduate certificates in Arts Administration & Cultural Management and Children's Mental Health.

She has worked in both film and television; has taught Musical Theatre to children and youth for eleven years; and has worked in senior roles for several not-for-profit organizations.

Lisa is excited to be launching the Arts Leadership Success Program, a high school credit course that teaches participants the skills outlined in *The Artistic Edge*.

To learn more about the programs offered by Canada's Academy of Stage and Studio Arts please reach out and connect:

www.stageandstudioarts.com
416-558-0922
info@stageandstudioarts.com

CPSIA information can be obtained at www.ICGtesting.com
Printed in the USA
BVOW01s0340210414

351101BV00003B/45/P